The Level Guide to the South West

howtobooks

Please send for a free copy of the latest catalogue to:
How To Books
3 Newtec Place, Magdalen Road
Oxford OX4 1RE, United Kingdom
Email: info@howtobooks.co.uk
www.howtobooks.co.uk

The Level Guide to the South West

The ONLY personally-assessed tourist guide for those with limited mobility

Peter Watts

howtobooks

Published by How To Books Ltd,
3 Newtec Place, Magdalen Road,
Oxford OX4 1RE. United Kingdom.
Tel: (01865) 793806. Fax: (01865) 248780
email: info@howtobooks.co.uk
www.howtobooks.co.uk

British Library Cataloguing in Publication Data.
A catalogue record for this book is available from the British Library.

Produced for How To Books by Deer Park Productions
Cover design by Baseline Arts Ltd, Oxford

Typesetting and design by Sparks – www.sparks.co.uk
Printed and bound in Great Britain by The Cromwell Press

Contents

This Book is for you

We hope it will help you get the most out of travelling around the South West of England.

We hope also that you will contact us with your feedback on places visited that are listed in the book. We want this book to become a consumer guide which reflects the actual experience of visitors such as you to attractions, shopping centres, places to stay and local places of interest throughout the South West. So, write in and give us the benefit of your experiences.

Peter is also writing a book to cover the whole of mainland UK, so your reports on places outside the South West will also be welcome. Accessibility for wheelchair users is key. Email Peter at enquiries@levelguides.net

And if you find correct contact details that differ from those in the book, please let us know so that we can put it right when we reprint. Email us on info@howtobooks.co.uk

The Publishers
www.howtobooks.co.uk

Note from the Author

It took me ages to admit I needed to use a wheelchair.

Having had MS for over twenty years I thought that if I started to use one of those contraptions it would be the end. The truth is it was actually the start – not of a wondrous new world, but a new start all the same.

So I began my new life as a 'sat down person'. Flushed with a newly found belief that the world is still out there to be taken – I decided to have a good look around. From lurching with walking sticks, which gave me an incredibly small world to play with, to one man and his wheelchair. I needed to check my boundaries, how much of this new world was available to me and the other estimated 750,000 wheelchair users. Obtaining a lottery grant I used the money to produce a small booklet detailing the accessibility of tourist attractions in the West Country. It was very popular and I realised people like me – seeing the world sat down – wanted more.

People who use wheelchairs are just like everyone else – it is just that we can't walk very well. My idea of a guide book with local history, places to visit, where to eat and drink, entertainment and places to stay was like any other guide book but seen through the eyes and needs of a wheelchair user.

I pitched the idea to Giles and Nikki at How To Books who have been very supportive as this book has taken shape. I hope you enjoy it and get the most out of the West Country – please let me know if you find good, accessible places so they can be included in future editions, and in the planned UK guide. Yes, this is only the start!

Peter Watts

WELCOME TO THE
SOUTH WEST

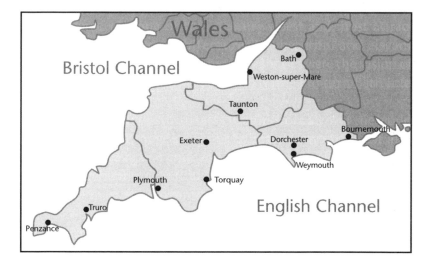

Somerset

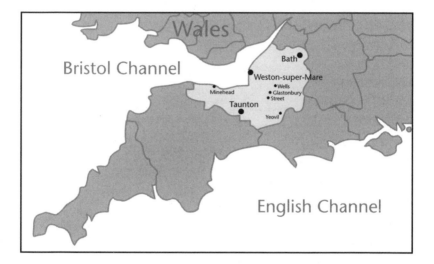

Wales

Bristol Channel

Bath
Weston-super-Mare
• Wells
Minehead • Glastonbury
• Street
Taunton
Yeovil

English Channel

The history

The old county of Somerset measures about 70 miles by 50 miles and lies on the southern shore of the Bristol Channel where the Brendon, Blackdown, Quantocks and Mendip hills guard the county.

The Romans withdrew from Somerset, and Britain, around AD 410 and the Celtic people reverted back to a largely rural existence. Without the order that the Romans brought to the county it was left to self-styled 'kings' to take control. King Cado, a cousin of King Arthur, is thought to have constructed a residence at South Cadbury and a stronghold at Dunster. Another high-status residence has been found at Glastonbury Tor and it is believed that this was the home to King Melwas who once kidnapped Queen Guinevere.

At first, the new Anglo-Saxon rulers took little notice of the Celts in the South-West but they did carry out raiding parties and there were many clashes between the Saxons and the Dumnonians.

In AD 680 King Ine of Wessex refounded the abbey at Glastonbury and this was joined by Muchelney in 693 and the minster at Wells in 705.

By AD 710, the armies of the Dumnonians were crushed and they withdrew further west with King Ine establishing a fortress at Taunton. Major excavations at Cheddar have revealed a great deal about Anglo-Saxon royal palaces and Saxon kings were frequent visitors to the county. King Edred died at his palace at Frome in 955 whilst his brother and nephew Kings Edmund and Edgar were both buried at Glastonbury.

Viking invaders caused massive damage. In 878 Alfred the Great was king, and close to defeat from the Vikings.

He was contemplating his next move when, staying with a peasant family, he burnt the cakes that he was supposed to be watching. It's not much of story but it is a famous one. Besides, he re-grouped and thrashed the Vikings.

By the 16th century the wetlands near Glastonbury had been drained and were now very valuable pasture for livestock, and lead and other mineral deposits were mined in the Mendips. In 1685, James, Duke of Monmouth landed at Lyme Regis and the ill-fated rebellion started. He quickly moved through Somerset adding to his army on the way with stops at Bridgwater, Glastonbury and Shepton Mallet. After the Battle of Sedgemoor where his men were cut down by horsemen, The Duke of Monmouth was captured and hung in July 1685.

Into the 18th century and poverty was rife. Farm work, the backbone of Somerset's economy, was becoming very insecure with the introduction of new machines which were seen as a threat to the workers' livelihoods. Emigration was a possibility and the government offered free passage to Australia or cheap fares to Quebec and New York.

However, by the 19th century Somerset towns were enjoying clean running water, sewage systems and improvements in medicine and housing.

The economy

From a population of just below 500,000 Somerset's economy is looking in a fairly healthy state. Unemployment is only 1.5%, with no great reliance on one major employer. Nor is there one significant town/city. The coast is popular – with Butlins at Minehead providing mostly seasonal jobs – and nearby Exmoor is a relaxing place to stay in the winter or summer and contrasts well with the harshness of Dartmoor in Devon or the bleakness of Bodmin Moor in Cornwall. The wicker weavers in the 'Somerset flats' provide interesting local products, mostly for tourists.

A debatable fact put out by the county council states that 44.4% of accommodation providers believe their accommodation is accessible to wheelchair users. From my own personal experience I would say the figure is more like 5–10%.

General

Somerset is still a rural, farming county but with great communications (M5), the inspiring sweep of Exmoor, the beauty of Bath and the inherent good natured ambience that makes a visit so worthwhile.

Taunton

Somerset's county town since 1843. A sensible look-ing town, functional rather than pretty. Set amongst some very fertile farmland on the river Tone. In the 8th century King Ine established a fortification here. A min-ster church was founded by the wife of Ine's successor – Queen Frithogyth. The town flourished, a mint was es-tablished and there were 64 burgesses in 1086. **Taunton Deane Manor** had ten mills at this time.

The town's first charter was granted in 1136 and a cas-tle was started by the bishop of Winchester in 1138. A market used to be held from 904 to 1929 in the triangle beside Fore Street right in the middle of the town. It now occupies a site at Priory Bridge Road.

There were two MPs from medieval times until 1884. Among its MPs were Thomas Cromwell (1529), and Henry Labouchere who resigned in 1859 to become the first and only Lord Taunton. During the Civil War the town was at first held for the Crown but later seized in 1644 by the Roundheads. In 1685, the Duke of Mon-mouth, after landing at Lyme Regis, was accommodated in a house in East Street. A group of 400 townsfolk joined him, but after defeat at Sedgemoor the rebels were either hanged without trial, or tried by Judge Jeffreys at his Bloody Assizes at the castle.

One of the oldest buildings is the **Tudor Tavern**, a restaurant, which dates back to the mid-14th century. In **East Street** are almshouses built in 1635 using brick, the earliest use of brick in the country.

Taunton Castle was the manor house for the bishops of Winchester. It also served as a courthouse. Since 1874 it housed the library and museum before Somerset County

Council took them over. In 1894 municipal buildings were constructed and, at the eastern part, Bishop Richard Fox of Winchester built the **Taunton Free Grammar School** in 1522. The castle is now a famous hotel and restaurant. TV chef Gary Rhodes used to be employed there. John Wesley preached in Taunton on a regular basis from 1743 and opened the Octagon Chapel off Middle Street in 1776. www.tauntondeane.gov.uk

Population

58,000

Parking

- OLD MARKET multi-storey – the main car park – is located at Paul Street.
- SHOPMOBILITY 01823 327900 is on the first floor of the Old Market car park and has its own parking area, which is free for disabled badge holders.

Toilets

There are two disabled toilets by the Old Market multi-storey car park (the one by TIC is a bit of a squeeze!)

Accommodation

- THE HOLIDAY INN, Deane Gate Avenue, Taunton. 01823 332222. Accessible, disabled parking and en-suite bedrooms. www.sixcontinentshotels.com
- HOLIDAY INN EXPRESS, Blackbrook Park, Taunton. 01823 624000. Accessible lodge accommodation, disabled parking and disabled en-suite bedrooms. www.hiexpress.com/taunton
- TRAVEL INN next to The White Lodge Beefeater, Bridgwater Road, Taunton. 01823 3211122.

Accessible en-suite bedrooms, disabled parking. www.travelinn.co.uk
- TRAVEL INN, Taunton Deane Motorway Services, M5 Southbound, Trull, Taunton. 01823 332228. www.travelinn.co.uk
- TRAVELODGE, Riverside Retail Park, Hankridge Farm, Blackbrook Park, Taunton. 0870 1911556. Accessible, disabled parking and en-suite bedrooms for disabled. www.travelodge.co.uk
- REDLANDS, Treble's Holford, Combe Florey, Taunton. 01823 433159. B&B and self-catering although the self-catering cottage has steps. But the B&B accommodation is very good and accessible. Parking close by on concrete. Large en-suite shower room. www.escapetothecountry.co.uk
- PROCTORS FARM, West Monkton, Taunton. 01823 412269. 17th century farmhouse with accessible B&B accommodation (roll in shower).
- HOLLY COTTAGE, Stoke St Gregory, Taunton. 01823 490828. Self-catering unit. One of five converted barns. Accessible, with roll in shower.
- PREMIER LODGE, Ilminster Road, Ruishton, Taunton. 0870 7001558. Next to the Blackbrook Tavern. Two en-suite bedrooms have facilities for disabled. www.premierlodge.co.uk

Caravan
- QUANTOCK ORCHARD CARAVAN PARK. 01984 618618. Ten miles west of Taunton. Hard standing for car, disabled toilet and bathroom.

Attractions

- TAUNTON RACECOURSE, Orchard Portman. Three miles south of Taunton on B3170 road to Honiton. Accessible.

- BREWHOUSE THEATRE AND ARTS CENTRE, Coal Orchard. 01823 283244. Disabled parking and auditorium seating, café and accessible toilets. www.brewhouse-theatre.co.uk
- SOMERSET COUNTY MUSEUM, Taunton Castle. 01823 320201. Only ground floor accessible.
- SOMERSET LEVELS BASKET AND CRAFT CENTRE. 01823 698688. Ten miles to the east. No particular facilities but it is level.
- SHEPPY'S CIDER FARM CENTRE, Bradford-on-Tone, Taunton. 01823 461233. Parking and disabled toilets. www.sheppyscider.com

Shopping

 Taunton is fairly level. **High Street** has a good number of shops and stores and is pedestrianised. As always, the older shops may have steps into them (including the post office!) but the bigger multi-branch shops usually have new shop fronts and are more level.

Under the main car park (Old Market multi-storey) is a new shopping centre, which links to the outside world at Fore Street and East Street. A wider-than-average pavement provides excellent access to High Street. Just beside the hot dog stall is **Bath Place**, a fascinating little snicket with several individual shops and a small café (step). It also connects to a car park (off **The Crescent**), which in turn gives access to a shopping arcade leading you back to High Street. In the centre of High Street are a number of bench seats. Fast food establishments (Burger King) are here together with the hot dog barrow.

Fore Street has a number of cafés and restaurants including Starbucks (coffee to stay awake with), which is accessible, but their toilets are not. County Stores in the town centre is definitely worth a visit – it seems to go on forever and sells good quality provisions and has the advantage of ramps throughout the shop. Debenhams is at the bottom of town and has a lift to all the floors including the self-service coffee shop.

For a pleasant walk/wheel travel to **Goodlands Gardens** at the rear of Debenhams and whizz alongside the Tone all the way to Tangiers – then double back to the County Museum, the Castle Hotel and on to the town centre.

A tour of the shops will take some time as it extends through North Street over the bridge and passes yet another small shopping centre. More individual shops are within a parade off St James Street. Also, if there is enough juice in the battery, visit **Vivary Park**, which is a lovely, level park at the southern end of the High Street. It is a delightful garden with many flowerbeds and a stream meandering through it. Over the bridge and you enter Vivary Park Golf and Tennis Club, a public golf course which is not only fairly short and level, it has two parking spaces for disabled drivers.

Out-of-town shopping is available at **Hankridge Farm** where there is a wide range of shops including and dominated by Sainsbury's with B&Q, Comet, Mothercare and many pubs and restaurants. Nearby is a drive-thru McDonald's, Hollywood Bowl tenpin bowling and a multi-screen cinema.

All these facilities are accessible using a wheelchair and most have dedicated parking for orange/blue badge holders.

Eating and drinking

 Two splendid bars are located in High Street (pedestrianised). One is Yates, which has a large bar area with disabled toilets – the other is the Toad At The Warehouse, which also has a very spacious bar serving drinks, coffee and very good and interesting food – definitely worth a visit. Disabled toilet.

Comment

Altogether, the town is good for access, the car parks are excellent and the majority of shops are available. *Highly recommended.*

Yeovil

Yeovil is a busy, thriving and expanding town. Well known for its association with **Westland Helicopters** which is its major employer. Before Westlands, however, the town was at the centre of the glove making and leather tanning industry. This provided Yeovil with prosperity from the 14th century until it collapsed in the 20th. In the 11th century the town is actually mentioned in the **Domesday Book** as Givele which sounds a lot more exotic then Yeovil. On the banks of the river Yeo, modern day Yeovil boasts a wide range of shopping facilities with its Quedam shopping centre but the centre is on a fairly steep slope and help will be needed if self-propelling! Alternatively there is a limited Shopmobility service 01935 475914. Car parks are all fairly central and there are lively outdoor markets on Tuesdays and Fridays.

Population

40,500

Parking

- HENDFORD car park is level into the main shopping areas.

Accommodation

- TRAVELODGE, Podimore (A303 near Ilchester). 01935 840074. Disabled parking and en-suite disabled bedrooms. www.travelodge.co.uk
- TRAVELODGE, Horton Cross, nr Ilminster. 08700 850950. Disabled parking and en-suite disabled bedrooms. www.travelodge.co.uk

- HORNSBURY MILL HOTEL AND INN, Chard. 01460 63317. Parking and disabled toilets.
- SHRUBBERY HOTEL, Ilminster. 01460 52108. Parking and disabled toilet. Ground floor bedrooms.

Camping
- LONG HAZEL INTERNATIONAL CARAVAN AND CAMPING, Sparkford. 01963 440002. Disabled facilities including adapted shower. www.sparkford.f9.co.uk/lhi.htm

Attractions
- YEOVILTON FLEET AIR ARM MUSEUM, Ilchester. 01935 840565. Excellent, large attraction. Accessible, level, café, disabled toilets and parking. www.fleetairarm.com
- FORDE ABBEY AND GARDENS, Chard. 01460 221290. Accessible gardens (but not Abbey). Disabled parking and toilets. Electric buggy available (a must!).
- HAYNES MOTOR MUSEUM, Sparkford, nr Yeovil. 01935 440804. Level, accessible museum. Very good facilities for wheelchairs. Parking, café and toilets. www.haynesmotormuseum.co.uk
- OCTAGON THEATRE, Hendford. 01935 422720. Parking. Disabled toilet, lift.
- BARRINGTON COURT (NT), Ilminster. 01460 241938. Tudor manor house. Accessible gardens plus buggy available. Accessible shop and restaurant. www.nationaltrust.org.uk
- MONTACUTE HOUSE (NT), Montacute. 01935 823289. Elizabethan house. Gardens, restaurant and shop accessible. Close parking. Many steps into house. www.nationaltrust.org.uk

- FISHING. Sutton Bingham Reservoir, Yeovil. 01935 872389
- CLAY PIGEON SHOOTING. Warden Hill. Eight miles south of Yeovil on A37 road to Dorchester.
- THE GARDENS NIGHTCLUB, Clarence Street. 01935 474569. Park in public car park close by. Disabled toilets.

Shopping

 The Quedam shopping centre has a good range of national and local shops. It is on a slope, so help will be needed. **Shopmobility** can provide a buggy. Telephone 01935 475914 to reserve a scooter. Denners, 25 High Street, department store is accessible and has a lift and café.

Middle Street also has numerous outlets and runs parallel to the Quedam.

Eating and drinking

- DENNERS department store. 01935 444444. Café and disabled toilets.
- McDONALD'S, restaurant and drive-thru, Lysander Road. Allocated parking and disabled toilets.
- SAFEWAY superstore, Lysander Road. Parking, café, disabled toilets.
- TESCO superstore, Huish. Parking, café and disabled toilets.
- THE BELL INN, Ash. 01935 823126. Pub and restaurant. Parking, level, disabled toilets.
- WINDWHISTLE INN AND RESTAURANT, Cricket St Thomas. 01460 30229. Level car park, accessible bars and disabled toilet.
- THE ARROW PUB, The Forum, Abbey Manor Park, Yeovil. 01935 476972. Level car park and adapted toilet.

- BREWSTERS PUB AND RESTAURANT, Alvington Avenue. 01935 476311. Level parking and disabled toilet.
- THE CROWN & VICTORIA, Farm Street, Tintinhull. 01935 823341. Car park, large beer garden, disabled toilet.
- COOPERS MILL, Hendford, Yeovil 01935 423878. Tarmac car park, ramped entrance, one or two steps inside. Disabled toilet.

Comment

Yeovil is a busy working town and it has many good shops. Unfortunately it is on a bit of a slope making manual (self-propelled) wheelchairs difficult to manoeuvre, but that only accounts for Middle Street and the area around Denners (Hendford) is accessible.

Weston-super-Mare

Weston-super-Mare is a very accessible seaside town and from its humble beginnings as a small 19th century fishing village of around a hundred souls it has blossomed into the county's largest seaside resort with a population of 70,000.

So many places in Somerset are called Weston so to distinguish it from the rest, 'super' (with lower case 's') was added (super meaning above) and Mare meaning sea in Latin. The Romans arrived and several pieces of pottery have been found, especially around the site of **Weston College**, where it is believed a Roman building once stood. Calamine was found in the mid-16th century at Worle Hill and was mined until the 19th century.

George III set the fashion for sea bathing at Weymouth in the late 18th century and the craze quickly caught on here. The first hotel appeared in 1810 (now The Royal Hotel) and a number of lodging houses followed.

Birnbeck Pier was built in 1867 for visitors to take the air and enjoy views towards Wales. A few years later a two mile promenade was constructed and in 1884 a through railway station opened up Weston to visitors and day-trippers. Visitors from Wales arrived also, from steamboats that docked at Birnbeck pier, which offered a vast array of entertainment. In 1904 a second pier was built closer to the town centre. In 1936 Weston Airfield opened and a lot of miners from South Wales would fly to Weston on their days off.

Population

70,000

Parking

- Level car parks are along Marine Parade (esplanade) and centrally sited around the town and at the railway station.
- SHOPMOBILITY 01934 420410 is at SOVEREIGN SHOPPING CENTRE multi-storey car park level 1.

Accommodation

- TRAVEL INN, Hutton Moor Road. 01934 622625. Next to The Pavilion Beefeater. Allocated parking and accessible en-suite bedrooms. www.travelinn.co.uk
- KINCLAVEN, 5 Park Place. 01934 645268. Seafront guesthouse. Accessible, lift, some bedrooms en-suite.
- DROVE ROAD HOSPITAL. Local MS Society owned mobile home. 01934 516279. Fully accessible.
- THE COMMODORE, Sand Bay. 01934 415778. Two ground floor bedrooms (1 double, 1 twin) in adjoining ramped annex are accessible – approx 60 yards distant. Level dining room with disabled toilet in reception.
- THE ROYAL HOTEL, South Parade. 01934 623601. Lift, ramp, some rooms are wide enough to cater for a wheelchair but no disabled bathroom.
- LAURISTON HOTEL, 6–12 Knightstone Road, Weston-super-Mare. 01934 620758. Seafront hotel that caters for visually impaired guests. Accessible throughout. Lift.

Attractions

- GRAND PIER. 01934 620238. Amusements, dodgems, cafés. Level and accessible.
- THE TIME MACHINE MUSEUM, Burlington Street. 01934 621028. Partly accessible (ground floor only). Café. Fabulous disabled toilets! www.n-somerset.gov.uk/museum

- INTERNATIONAL HELICOPTER MUSEUM, Weston Heliport, Weston-super-Mare. 01934 635227. Accessible and adapted toilet. www.helicoptermuseu m.freeserve.co.uk
- SEA LIFE CENTRE, Marine Parade. 01934 613 361. Level Access.
- ODEON CINEMA, The Centre. 08705 050007. Ground floor access only.
- HORSE WORLD, Whitchurch, nr Bristol. 01275 540173. Accessible, tea room, parking and disabled toilets.
- THE PLAYHOUSE AND WINTER GARDENS. 01934 645544. Park in Sovereign car park. Level walk to Playhouse, ramp to foyer and lift to stalls. Disabled toilet.

Shopping

- SOVEREIGN SHOPPING CENTRE, High Street. Over 40 retail shops, Burger King restaurant/café, Marks & Spencer, Wilkinsons, New Look, Dixons etc. … Shopmobility. Car park. Lift. Disabled toilet.
- WINTERSTOKE COMMERCIAL CENTRE. Asda, parking, café, toilets. Focus, parking. Staples, parking. McDonald's restaurant with toilets and drive-thru takeaway.
- TESCO, town centre/esplanade store, disabled parking (well administered by a private security company to keep out non disabled), café and toilets, fast card petrol station, 3 cash machines. It's all a bit frenetic and claustrophobic but it is nice to see those selfish ABs unceremoniously moved on when they try to nick disabled parking places.

Eating and drinking

- McDONALD'S restaurant/café. Disabled toilets.

● WESTON FLIPPER, fish and chips restaurant and takeaway. 4 St James Street. 01934 626206. Disabled street parking outside – excellent fish and chips.

Comment

Weston-super-Mare is a very pleasant place and flat. There is a nice feeling of space about the town and it is one of the most accessible.

Minehead

Minehead was first mentioned in the Domesday Book of 1087. There was a Celtic settlement here and it is probably from their name for the hill that sheltered the colony 'Mynydd' which leads us to Minehead. It wasn't until the 15th century that the fishing trade was developed when a trading route to Ireland was established. In 1791 a massive fire destroyed much of the town. The two stone buildings, **Bampton House** and the Almshouses, that did survive can still be seen today. In the 19th century, with the arrival of the railway, the town became a holiday resort with expansion and much new building for the visitors took place. Sir Billy Butlin built his holiday camp in the post-war era and it is still there today.

The town is flat and fairly accessible with very few hills.

Population

11,670

Accommodation

- THE PROMENADE HOTEL, The Esplanade. 01643 702572. John Grooms Holidays – 8 of 12 bedrooms and all public rooms accessible.
- PERITON PARK HOTEL, Middlecombe. 01643 706885. Country house hotel on edge of Exmoor. Accessible bedrooms with spacious en-suite bathroom. Two steps for main entrance.
- PRIMROSE HILL, Wood Lane, Blue Anchor. 01643 821200. Four accessible bungalows. Private gardens.

- WESTERMILL FARM, EXFORD. 01643 831238. Two Scandinavian log cabins on working farm. Built for disabled access.

Camping
- BEECHES HOLIDAY PARK, Blue Anchor Bay. 01984 640391. Two bedroom holiday home suitable for wheelchair user.

Attractions

- THE BEACH. Very wide esplanade gives access to the beach. The esplanade itself is very accessible having parking and a flat long stretch of tarmac to wheel on. At one end is Butlins and the other the town centre.
- DUNSTER CASTLE (NT). 01643 821314. Dates back to Norman times but restored by Victorians to their image of how castles should look. Access is difficult but can be managed with strong help. The village itself is a delight – best to try and park in the centre as the car park is a little way off and the place is only small. www.nationaltrust.org.uk
- HOLNICOTE ESTATE (NT). 01643 862452 Walks across Exmoor and to bird hide which has been adapted for disabled. Telephone for details of most accessible. www.nationaltrust.org.uk
- BUTLINS. Family entertainment resort – day visitors welcomed and the whole site is accessible. 01643 703331. www.butlins.co.uk
- BAKELITE MUSEUM, Orchard Mill, Bridge Street, Williton. 01984 632133. For all things about Bakelite! Set in an old Mill. Art Deco exhibits, café. www.thebakelitemuseum.co.uk
- EXMOOR FALCONRY AND ANIMAL FARM, Allerford, Porlock. 01643 862816. www.exmoorfalconry.co.uk

- WEST SOMERSET RAILWAY, The Railway Station, Minehead. 01643 704996. Lovely coastal run from Minehead to Bishops Lydeard. Good access with specially adapted coach for wheelchair users and disabled RADAR toilets at Minehead and Bishops Lydeard. www.west-somerset-railway.co.uk

Shopping

The neat town centre has a number of accessible shops but this is a small seaside town so the facilities are only to be expected.

Tesco is located on the eastern side and has parking, a café, disabled toilets and a fast card petrol station.

Eating and drinking

- TESCO with parking and toilets.
- VARIOUS TEA ROOMS/COFFEE SHOPS throughout the town and some have outdoor seating.
- McDONALD'S restaurant and drive-thru with disabled parking and toilets.

Comment

Exmoor's seaside resort is famous for the **Butlins Somerwestworld.** If you do not want to stay there you can purchase just a day ticket. It is accessible but you are not allowed out after dark!

Exmoor is there to be explored and there are some great, accessible places within the **Exmoor National Park.** The National Trust provides a good service for wheelchair users and the newly adapted bird hide and easy access trails are worth a look at.

Glastonbury

The mystical, ancient town of Glastonbury is the capital of the Isle of Avalon and the unofficial New Age capital of England. Druids, pagan worship, King Arthur, Goddess Conferences, Knights of The Round Table are all here, along with just about every alternative medicine around. There is a tale of Joseph of Arimathea burying two cruets filled with the blood and sweat of the dying Jesus somewhere in Glastonbury. The **Holy Thorn Bush** was said to have been established when Joseph went ashore after docking his ship nearby and placed his staff on the ground where it instantly took root. The Holy Thorn (protected in a cage) blossoms at Christmas and a sprig is cut and sent to the monarch every year. Joseph is also said to have brought a chalice from which Jesus drank at the Last Supper – the cup, the Holy Grail, is buried at the foot of the Tor.

Glastonbury Tor rises to 518ft above sea level and used to be accessed by ship. It is above an area of marshland that periodically was flooded by the sea. Even as recently as 1607, when the sea walls were breached, the sea was lapping at the foot of the Tor.

King Edgar, the first king of a united England, died and was buried at Glastonbury. The ruins that you see today are mainly of the church built after the 1184 fire. The site of the supposed tomb of Arthur and Guinevere is marked in the grass. The town is a place of Christian pilgrimage and both the Anglican and Catholic Churches hold their own summer pilgrimages in the Abbey grounds.

Whatever you choose to believe, go to Glastonbury and soak up the atmosphere – it's different!

Of course the other event Glastonbury is world famous for is the **annual festival** on Michael Eavis's Worthy Farm, Pilton.

Population

8,700

Accommodation

- HIGHLAND STUDIO, Highlands Guest House, 21 Rowley Road, Glastonbury. 01458 834587. Halfway up the Tor but this property is very accessible.
- BURCOTT MILL, Wookey, Wells. 01749 673118. Very attractive former watermill offering modern, comfortable accommodation with one accessible bedroom and shower room. www.burcottmill.com

Camping

- ISLE OF AVALON TOURING CARAVAN PARK. 01458 833618. Large disabled toilet.

Attractions

- GLASTONBURY ABBEY, Abbey Gatehouse. 01458 832267. 'Oldest Christian Church'. Majority accessible including shop and café. Wheelchairs available on site. Disabled toilet. www.glastonburyabbey.com
- SOMERSET RURAL LIFE MUSEUM, Abbey Farm, Glastonbury. 01458 834684. Partly accessible attraction depicting life in the 19th century. Disabled toilets.
- PEAT MOORS CENTRE, Westhay, Glastonbury. 01458 860246. Partly accessible prehistoric journey about the Somerset Levels and Wetlands. Disabled toilet. www.somerset.gov.uk/levels/pmvc.htm
- GLASTONBURY TOR. Yes, it's very difficult to climb to the top of this majestic and mystical hill but it can

be made and if your helper is very strong, patient and loving, the king of the fairies, Gwyn ap Nudd, will welcome you as you enter his home!

Shopping

The main shopping street is on a bit of a slope so it would be advisable to take someone along with you to help push. The shops are an occultist's dream, with potions and lotions to cure just about anything. Courses to become a Druid Goddess are held on a regular basis (usually during the summer months) and you can learn of the 'psychic war effort' that helped during World War II. If he's not in jail, seek out Free Rob Cannabis who has a shop in the town.

Comment

It is like nowhere else – late middle aged men wobbling around with their thinning grey hair tied in a pony tail and stick thin women of a certain age dressed in long, flowery, flowing cheese cloth dresses. In the shops and market stalls the overriding heady smell is one of joss sticks and cannabis.

Go to Glastonbury with an open mind – it really is an incredible place.

Street

Named after the ancient causeway running across the **River Brue**. There is evidence of a pre-Saxon settlement at Street and the Celtic saint, St Gildas, was a resident and founded a church here, but apart from that there is little in the way of Street history. The town has grown up in the shadow of Glastonbury (it used to be part of the Abbey's estate). Street is now famed for its association with the independent school **Millfield** which was started in 1935. The school has produced many famous sporting old boys and has close links with Somerset County Cricket Club.

The area has always been a place for the tanning industry and the town's other famous connection is C and J Clark. The brothers Cyrus and James, the sons of a local Quaker, formed their company in 1825 making slippers from sheepskin. In the 21st century the shoe company, which has its headquarters in the town, is still going strong and in 1993 the **Clarks Village** factory outlet opened. There are over 50 retail units here and they are all accessible. There are cafés, takeaways, barrows selling baked potatoes and crêpes and as it is on the doorstep of Street you can wheel into the town and have a look around the town. Disabled toilets by the entrance and Shopmobility are here on 01458 840064.

Population

 11,000

Accommodation

- WESSEX HOTEL, High Street, Street 01458 443383. Step or ramp into entrance and one step into public rooms. Lift but no adaptations. www.wessexhotel.com

Attractions

- MUCHELNEY ABBEY (EH). 01458 250664. Two miles south of Langport. Remains of 8th century Benedictine Abbey. Accessible. www.english-heritage.org.uk
- SHOE MUSEUM, C&J Clark Ltd, 40 High Street. 01458 842169. Two steps up into attraction but after that it is fairly level. Café.
- MOORLYNCH VINEYARD, Street. 01458 210393. Wine making in Somerset. Guided tour of vines and winemaking process. Parking, restaurant, shop, and disabled toilet. www.moorlynch.com

Shopping

- CLARKS FACTORY OUTLET VILLAGE is a great success. Well over 50 shops are here and so is Shopmobility 01458 840064. Allocated parking. Café/restaurant and takeaways. ATM. Leads directly into the town, which is level. Disabled toilets (RADAR).

> **Comment**
>
> Street, Wells and Glastonbury are all very close together and if you are visiting one of these towns you might as well visit all three. Street is the flattest and the most wheelchair friendly.

Wells

Wells has been a settlement since neolithic times. Water from underground Mendip streams surface here and several springs fizz into a pool to the east of the cathedral. The Saxon King Ine was the patron of Wells' first church, which was founded by St Aldhelm around 700 AD. Two hundred years later Athelm was appointed bishop and Wells' status was raised to Cathedral Church. In 1180 Bishop Reginald de Bolun pulled down the old cathedral and began building a new one, which took 250 years to complete. The magnificent West Front has about 400 carved figures. In 1986 during a service on the green a new statue of the Risen Christ was unveiled in the presence of the Prince of Wales.

High up in the north transept is an incredible mechanical clock that dates from 1392 – the second oldest in England after Salisbury.

Famous Bishops of Wells include Thomas Wolsey who, after failing to secure Henry VIII's divorce from Catherine of Aragon, was accused of treason and accordingly died.

Most parts of the cathedral are accessible with a wheelchair, with ramps for access at the northwest door. A wheelchair is available for loan. Wells Cathedral School is a well-established private school with musical leanings and is situated within the Cathedral grounds.

Wells is England's smallest city, it is neat, quiet and very attractive with some splendid architecture, all built up around the cathedral, which dominates the city.

Population

10,400

Accommodation

- HENLEY HILL FARM, Haybridge, Wells. 01749 678972. Ground floor bedroom with en-suite large shower. Working farm. www.henleyhillfarm.co.uk
- DOUBLE-GATE FARM HOLIDAYS, Double-Gate Farm, Godney, Wells. 01458 832217. One ground floor, twin en-suite bedroom with very large bathroom for the disabled. www.doublegatefarm.com

Attractions

- THE BISHOP'S PALACE, The Henderson Rooms, The Bishop's Palace, Wells. Close to the cathedral, the early part of the palace dates from the 13th century. A pair of mute swans ring the gatehouse bell for food (this all but died out because of visitors feeding the swans but the swans are now being re-trained to perform their party piece). www.wellscathedral.org.uk

Shopping

A shop at West Cloister at the cathedral sells various goods.

A good range of shops for day-to-day living are available in the city and there is limited on-street parking. Somerfield supermarket has a store near the centre. Most of the town is fairly accessible with only mild inclines. The pretty market place has a market on Wednesdays and Saturdays.

Eating and drinking

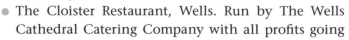

- The Cloister Restaurant, Wells. Run by The Wells Cathedral Catering Company with all profits going to assist the cathedral in its work. Morning coffee, lunches and teas. Accessible.

Comment

Very impressive cathedral that *is* Wells. The delightful Cathedral Green fronts the West Front and if you can visit this part of the city (no cars) do so.

Bath

Bath was established as a town in AD 43 after the Roman invasion of Britain. The city's fortune has ever since revolved around its hot thermal springs and the ensuing tourism they attract.

Legend has it that well before the Roman invasion, and before he was king, Bladud founded the town and discovered the springs and their medicinal properties. Because he had leprosy he'd been banished to the Avon valley to keep pigs and one day, as the pigs emerged from a steamy swamp, their skin diseases had gone. He joined them in the swamp and his leprosy disappeared as well.

The Romans called the town Aquae Sulis after the Celtic goddess Sul. The **temple and baths** were developed over the following centuries. Cleanliness was an important part of Roman life and you can imagine somebody going into the changing room and then proceeding via a cold plunge through a sequence of hot and cold rooms, both dry and wet. Along the way, oil was rubbed into the body as the pores would be open and then another cold plunge bath would serve to close up the pores.

As the Romans left the town declined and the Saxons captured it in 577. It was they who changed the name to Bath. A monastery was founded and this brought Bath much needed renewed fame. The coronation of the first king of England, Edgar, took place at the abbey church in 973. After the Norman Conquest, **Bath Abbey** became a cathedral and was rebuilt on a much grander scale.

Henry VIII closed the monastery in the 1530s but it didn't hit Bath too badly.

Taking to the hot waters became very fashionable and a cure for various ailments including aiding the conception of a child, which worked for Queen Anne. As a result, by the 18th century, Bath was at the height of fashion and drew admirers from the arts (Thomas Gainsborough, Henry Fielding, Jane Austen), the military (Lord Nelson, General Wade) and political life (William Pitt), not to mention numerous aristocrats and members of the royal family.

Apart from the unique hot springs Bath is, of course, home to some of this country's best and most attractive **Georgian architecture**. The beautiful and elegant crescents, streets, squares and circuses were the vision of the architect John Wood who wanted to turn Bath into a Roman city.

Nowadays Bath attracts visitors from all over the world and has a range of shops to match anywhere – it also seems to have a coffee shop on every street corner, from the ubiquitous Starbucks to every other coffee franchise. Even in the **covered market**, which in other towns would resemble a car boot sale without the car boots, Bath has stalls with unusual coffees and teas to try. It must be a city that never sleeps.

Population

87,000

Parking

There is a labyrinthine network of roads throughout Bath centre with many parking spaces to be found but if you are not brave enough for that use the car parks by the bus station. The HAM MULTI-STOREY is very central and if displaying a disabled blue/orange badge, parking is free. There aren't many spaces for disabled but there is a lift so any will do.

Accommodation

- HOLIDAY INN EXPRESS, Lower Bristol Road, Brougham Hayes. 0870 4442792. Seven fully adapted rooms for disabled both ground floor and first floor. Above average lodge accommodation offering larger than normal shower rooms. Lift. www.hiexpress.com
- TRAVEL LODGE, George Street. 0870 850950. Four fully adapted bedrooms with en-suite bathrooms. Lift. www.travelodge.co.uk
- THE HILTON, Walcot Street. 01225 463411. One fully adapted en-suite bedroom. Lift.
- THE BATH SPA HOTEL, Sydney Road. 0870 4008222. Two fully adapted ground floor en-suite bedrooms.
- DUKES HOTEL, Great Pulteney Street. 01225 787960. One fully adapted ground floor en-suite bedroom. Three steps into hotel and assistance can be given.
- THE ABBEY HOTEL, North Parade. 01225 461603. One fully adapted en-suite bedroom.
- THE CARFAX HOTEL, Great Pulteney Street. 01225 462089. One fully adapted en-suite bedroom.
- MENZIES WATERSIDE HOTEL, Rossiter Road. 01225 338855. One fully adapted en-suite bedroom.

Guest house and hotels with ground floor rooms but no adaptations
- THE AYRLINGTON HOTEL, Pulteney Road. 01225 425495. Two rooms accessible via side door with ramp.
- THE ROYAL HOTEL, Manvers Street. 01225 463134. All rooms accessible by lift but no adaptations.
- THE FRANCIS HOTEL, Queens Square. 0870 4008223. Rooms accessible via lift but no special adaptations.

- PARADISE HOUSE, Holloway. 01225 317723. No adapted rooms but ground floor rooms accessible with assistance.
- HAUTE COMBE HOTEL, Newbridge Road. 01225 420061. One ground floor room accessible, but bathroom not accessible with wheelchair.
- HIGHWAYS HOUSE, Wells Road. 01225 421238. One ground floor room accessible with minor assistance (one step).
- ASHLEY VILLA HOTEL, Newbridge Road. 01225 421683. Four ground floor rooms accessible with assistance (two steps).
- POLDEN COURT, University of Bath, Bath. 01225 826622. Four bedrooms designed for wheelchair users, two have roll-in showers. Sloped entrance. Ramp to restaurant.

Attractions

- BATH ABBEY, Bath. 01225 422462. Accessible.
- THE MUSEUM OF EAST ASIAN ART, Bath. 01225 464640. Wheelchair access to all floors via lift.
- ROMAN BATHS, Pump Room, Stall Street, Bath. 01225 477785. Level access to inner and outer terraces only. Audio guide. www.romanbaths.co.uk
- MUSEUM OF COSTUME, Assembly Rooms, Bennett Street, Bath. 01225 444793. www.museumofcostume. co.uk
- PRIOR PARK GARDENS (NT), Ralph Allen Drive, Bath. 01225 833422. Fine example of landscape gardens from 18th century. Disabled toilet. www.nationaltrust.org.uk
- THE GUILDHALL, Bath. 01225 477724. 18th century banqueting room with neo-classical decoration.

- FARLEIGH HUNGERFORD CASTLE (EH), Farleigh Hungerford, Bath. 01225 754026. Accessible 14th century castle ruins. www.english-heritage.org.uk
- VICTORIA ART GALLERY, Bridge Street, Bath. 01225 477232. Substantial collection by Gainsborough, Turner and Sickert. Accessible. www.victoriagal.org.uk

Shopping

Fantastic range of shops – there's even a branch of Geives & Hawkes. Redevelopment of the centre has opened up certain areas and these have been made into rather select alleys and alleyways, and always with a coffee shop or two. Strange that when mooching around the centre and rubbing shoulders with designer labels and trendy, high fashion and high expense shops, you come across a Spar shop – it looks totally out of place but quite reassuring.

Eating and drinking

Accessible town centre pubs include:

- ALL BAR ONE, 11–13 High Street, Bath. 01225 324021. One ground floor room, level access and level inside. Large bar. Disabled toilet.
- RAT & PARROT, 38 Westgate Street, Bath. 01225 461642. Ramped access to bar. Disabled toilet.
- THE SLUG & LETTUCE, Unit 1, York Buildings, George Street. Level access with large bar area and disabled toilet.
- THE LITTERN TREE, 23 Milsom Street, Bath 01225 310772. Lift to first floor and toilets but no disabled adaptations.
- HARVESTER LAMBRIDGE, Gloucester Road, Bath 01225 443344 Disabled parking and disabled toilet.
- CAFFÈ NERO, level access. Excellent Panini.

- LE PARISSIENNE, French style café/restaurant, eat in or takeaway.
- STARBUCKS, accessible.
- SHIRES YARD. Cafés and shops over two floors (no lift).
- PAVILION SHOPPING CENTRE, Madisons coffee shop and snacks, accessible – *recommended*.
- Also within Pavilion Shopping Centre is WAITROSE SUPERMARKET.

Comment

Unusually for such an old town and one that is on something of a slope, it actually is fairly accessible. A fabulous place that just has to be visited, time and again.

Dorset

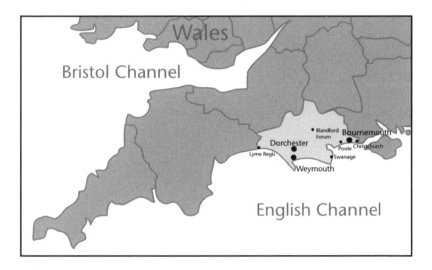

The history

A few million years ago dinosaurs roamed in West Dorset. Relics and fossils of their time here are thrown up at the well-known 'fossil hunters' spot of Lyme Regis beach. Sifting through the rocks at Lyme or nearby Charmouth is not very wheelchair friendly but a shop is open in the town to view or buy the fossils. There are also several museums that have fossilised remains on show.

The dramatic coastline once proved a valuable source of income for pirates and smugglers. Now it is the turn of donkey rides, amusements and beach activities. From the early days it has been home to all manner of seafaring folk with its wide and sheltered bays and it contains the world's largest natural harbour at Poole.

Trawling through history, the county appears to have been invaded by just about any passing, marauding group taking a fancy to the lush downlands. The Romans, however, were the biggest influence and after defeating the Durotriges, who inhabited Maiden Castle, established what is now Dorchester, the county town. They named the town Durnovaria but the next raiders – the Saxons, changed it again.

The economy

The economy of Dorset is a combination of agriculture, tourism and modern industry such as the Weymouth headquarters of the fashion clothing retailer, New Look. Barclays International is based in Poole as is Sunseeker

– boat builders for the seriously financially comfortable. To the south east of the county is Europe's largest on-shore oilfield at Wytch Farm, and Moore's Dorset Knob biscuits can be found at Morecombelake. The decline in agriculture as an occupation is well documented and easy to see. With farms of 2,000 acres managed by a small handful of workers, only 3% of the county population are actually employed in agriculture. There is a large number of big landowners and estates. The Duchy of Cornwall possesses a major chunk, especially around Dorchester where Prince Charles' vision of modern living, Poundbury Village, is taking shape.

Dorset is a pleasant place to live and work, enjoying a fairly mild climate, and is around two to two-and-a-half hours from London, either by train or car.

The invading armies of today are much more aggressive than those of yesteryear (you try pinching a parking space on Weymouth seafront in August!), and like previous invaders they provide stability and jobs. Dorset's tourism supports about 25,000 people and is the third most popular county in England in terms of nights stayed in local accommodation.

General

Dorset measures about 60 miles by 40 miles and is one of the smallest counties in the country. Yet it incorporates in its green and fertile land all the varied aspects found elsewhere in the country, but not a millimetre of motorway.

Population is about 665,000, and Poole and Bournemouth account for nearly half of this, but occupy only a fraction in terms of area. The county has an attractive and dramatic coastline with safe, sandy beach resorts at Weymouth, Swanage, Poole, Studland and Bournemouth to the east. To the west, the unique 20-mile pebble bank – Chesil Beach – runs from Portland to West Bay with the pebbles decreasing in size as it travels west. UNESCO has recently awarded World Heritage site status for the entire length of the West Dorset coastline.

Dorchester

The county town of Dorset and the administration centre for public services. In AD 43 the Roman Army marched into town, conquered the natives (the Durotriges) at **Maiden Castle** and founded a new town (Durnovaria). The neolithic henge, **Maumbury Rings**, used to be used for pagan worship and the odd hanging. The Romans adapted it to an amphitheatre.

Thomas Hardy is the town's most famous export and his presence is everywhere. He was born about three miles away at **Higher Bockhampton** in 1840 and he died in 1928. Both the place of his birth and his last home, which he designed, are owned by the National Trust and available to be viewed.

Dorchester's other claim to fame (apart from being christened the meanest town in Britain because of their Christmas lights, or lack of them) is **Judge Jeffreys Bloody Assizes**. On 11 September 1685 after a fruitless attempt to overthrow James II, some of the Duke of Monmouth's band of followers were tried at The Antelope Hotel (now a shopping arcade) and 110 were convicted and hanged.

Other noteworthy figures from the past include **Lawrence of Arabia** who lived at his cottage, **Clouds Hill**, just outside Bovington. The cottage is owned by the National Trust but is impossible to enter in a wheelchair. The **Tolpuddle Martyrs** (five miles east) are commemorated every year and union bosses and politicians join a symbolic march through the village.

The Duchy of Cornwall owns large amounts of Dorset including farms surrounding the town. On the western outskirts is Prince Charles' popular new housing development, **Poundbury**. In total about 200 acres will be developed over the next 20 years.

Population

 15,000

Accommodation

- WARMWELL HOLIDAY PARK, Dorchester (four miles east). 01305 852911. Log cabins with limited facilities – disabled toilet at reception.
- TAMARISK FARM, West Bexington (seven miles west). 01308 89774. Cottage on organic farm designed/ adapted for disabled. www.tamariskfarm.co.uk
- THE KINGCOMBE CENTRE, Toller Porcorum (six miles north-west). 01300 320684. Two bedrooms designed for disabled. www.kingcombecentre.co.uk

Attractions

- KEEP MILITARY MUSEUM, Bridport Road, Dorchester. 01305 264066. Accessible museum about the history of Devon and Dorset regiment. Free rear parking. Lift. Disabled toilet. www.keepmilitarymuseum.org
- TUTANKHAMUN EXHIBITION, High West Street, Dorchester. 01305 269571. Popular ground floor exhibition. Two steps up for access – ramp available. No disabled toilets or parking.
- MAIDEN CASTLE (EH), Dorchester. Important neolithic site established about 3,000 BC and extending to around 45 acres. It's free and accessible but help required. Compacted paths.
- THE TANK MUSEUM, Bovington, Bere Regis 01929 405096 Excellent, level museum about tanks. New displays. Café, shop and allocated parking. Disabled toilets. *Recommended*. www.tankmuseum.co.uk

- THORNCOMBE WOODS AND THOMAS HARDY'S BIRTH PLACE, Higher Bockhampton, Dorchester. Very pleasant council owned woods, which are partly wheelchair accessible. Within the woods is Hardy's cottage (NT) but only the gardens are accessible. Help needed. www.nationaltrust.org.uk
- ATHELHAMPTON HOUSE, Puddletown. 01305 848363. Most attractive 15th century manor house. Lovely Grade 1 listed gardens. Accessible. Restaurant. Adapted disabled toilet. www.athelhampton.co.uk

Shopping

Pedestrianised main shopping street (**South Street**). Three shopping arcades – **Hardye** arcade leads to main car park (Charles Street), which is level and has toilets. **Tudor** arcade leads to Waitrose supermarket.

Most of the town shops (Boots, Woolworths, WH Smith, Post Office etc) are accessible. Goulds Department Store has wheelchair access, a lift, excellent café and disabled toilets.

Out-of-town shopping
A small retail development comprising Tesco, Currys, Allied Carpets and Halfords is located along Weymouth Avenue. Tesco is a 24hr store and has disabled parking, café and disabled toilets.

Eating and drinking

Dorchester is awash with coffee/tea shops and most are accessible.

- THE TRUMPET MAJOR (pub), Allington Avenue, Dorchester. 01305 262091. Total access. Large car park and beer garden. Open all day and disabled toilets.

- THE JUNCTION HOTEL (pub), 42 Great Western Rd, Dorchester. 01305 755000. Lively town centre pub. Some steps. Ramp for side entrance. Adapted disabled toilet.
- THE SUN INN (pub), Lower Burton, Charminster. 01305 250445. One mile north of Dorchester. Allocated parking. Accessible. Adapted toilet.

Comment

Dorchester is better known these days for Prince Charles' vision of modern living at Poundbury, his model village. But the town is accessible and the centre is flat although help will be needed if venturing onto High West or High East Street.

Weymouth

Weymouth is actually two towns, Melcombe Regis and Weymouth, occupying opposite sides of the River Wey. **Melcombe Regis** is the larger of the two and is the centre of today's town but Weymouth, occupying the southern side of the river, was the chosen name when they amalgamated by order of Elizabeth I in 1571. In 1348 a ship from Bristol brought with it 'the seeds of the terrible pestilence' infecting and ultimately halving the population – it was the first time the **Black Death** had arrived on British shores.

On a brighter note, the town really came of age when loopy George III visited Weymouth to recover from illness and returned frequently until about 1805. He single-handedly put the town on the map and started the craze for sea bathing. The Court brought the place prosperity, celebrity and prominence.

A chalk figure representing the King was carved out on the steep hills at **Osmington** but it displeased the king because it showed him leaving Weymouth and he liked the town.

Population

46,000

Accommodation

- LODMOOR TRAVEL INN. 01305 767964. Two disabled en-suite bedrooms. Car park. www.travelinn.co.uk
- HOTEL REMBRANDT, 12 Dorchester Rd, Weymouth. 01305 764000. No specific bedrooms for disabled but

the whole hotel is accessible with ramp at rear and disabled toilet. Car park, leisure suite/pool.

- HOTEL CENTRAL, Maiden Street, Weymouth. 01305 760700. Three ground floor bedrooms for disabled but no specific facilities. Town centre. Parking.
- ANCHOR HOUSE, Holland Road. 01446 771311. John Grooms Holidays. Adapted house for disabled. Lift.

Caravans
- CHESIL BEACH HOLIDAY PARK, Portland Rd. 01305 773233. Has caravans adapted for wheelchair users.
- WEYMOUTH BAY (HAVEN) PARK, Preston. 01305 8322271. Has caravans adapted for wheelchair users.
- LITTLESEA (HAVEN) HOLIDAY PARK. 01202 886022. Has caravans adapted for wheelchair users.
- BAGLAKE FARM, Litton Cheney (three miles west). 01308 482222. Adapted cottage for three people.

Attractions
- LODMOOR COUNTRY PARK (well signposted). Variety of attractions including pitch and putt, mini railway, go-karts, Model World and Sea World, all of which are accessible. There's a snack bar, which is ramped.
- BREWERS QUAY. Former brewery converted into imaginative speciality shopping centre. Car park with two disabled spaces. Level into centre. 20 shops over 2 floors. Lift. Café. *Recommended.* Excellent disabled toilets.
- SHARKEY'S DEEP SEA ADVENTURE, 9 Custom House Quay. 01305 760690. Accessible attraction with lift to all floors. Disabled toilet.

- THE LAKESIDE SUPERBOWL, St Nicholas Street, Weymouth. 01305 781444. Tenpin bowling. Accessible. Disabled toilet.
- THE NOTHE FORT, Barrack Road, Weymouth. 01305 787243. 16th century building, 12 gun batteries, 70 rooms. Help required – 70% available to wheelchair user. Parking for disabled, tearooms, and disabled toilet all within the fort. Fantastic views. After visiting the fort, wheel around the **Nothe Gardens** – great views over Portland Harbour and Weymouth Bay.
- CINEWORLD CINEMA, town centre – next to Debenhams. 01305 768759. Accessible nine-screen cinema. Disabled toilet.
- GALA BINGO, 18 Crescent Street, Weymouth. 01305 785180. Wheelchair access and disabled toilet.

Shopping

Weymouth town centre has recently had some much needed, major rebuilding work and now, after a 23-year absence, it sees the return of Debenhams. The piazza has several shops, including Debenhams and all have total access.

The new work has left Weymouth with an excellent range of accessible shops.

Eating and drinking

- THE LODMOOR BREWERS FAYRE, Preston Beach Road, Weymouth. 01305 767964. Next to public car park. Excellent, accessible pub with disabled toilet.
- THE SPA, 229 Dorchester Road, Radipole Spa, Weymouth. 01305 785231. Allocated disabled parking. Accessible pub and restaurant.
- THE WHITE HART, Lower Bond Street, Weymouth. 01305 785165. Level access from piazza. Adapted toilet.

- THE TOAD AT THE BANK, 62 St Thomas Street, Weymouth. 01305 830195. Level access. Good food and disabled toilets.
- THE SWAN INN, 41–43 St Thomas Street, Weymouth. 01305 750231. Large Weatherspoon pub with disabled toilet (RADAR).
- THE RECTORY, St Thomas Street, Weymouth. Morning coffee to nightclub. Attractive, period town centre building with great outside personal lift. Interesting food. Disabled toilets.
- DEBENHAMS CAFÉ, lift to first floor café. Toilets (RADAR). Great position, overlooking the inner harbour – sit and watch the gasometer rust.

Comment

Weymouth has changed over the last ten years and all for the better. It is now one of the finest and most accessible towns in Dorset. Parking is a problem (not enough spaces).

Lyme Regis

The town's major landmark is **The Cobb**, an artificial harbour and breakwater that was originally detached from the mainland and only joined in the 18th century. Lyme Regis used to be a very important and busy port enjoying a brisk and profitable trade with the Americas and the Mediterranean. It is said that in the 18th century it was larger than the port of Liverpool. In 1685 the Duke of Monmouth landed at Lyme Regis and started his ill-fated Monmouth Rebellion. Twenty three rebels were hung and quartered on the beach after it failed. John Fowles lives in the town and his book *The French Lieutenant's Woman* was filmed here. The area is very popular with fossil hunters.

Population

3,500

Accommodation

- BINGHAMS FARM, Melplash. 01308 488234. Holiday flat designed for disabled.
- RUDGE FARM, Chilcombe. 01308 482630. Converted and accessible barns. www.rudgefarm.co.uk
- WEST BAY HOLIDAY PARK, West Bay. 01308 422424. Adapted caravans for disabled.
- THE POPLARS, Wood Farm Caravan Park, Charmouth. 01297 560697. One apartment adapted for disabled.
- STABLE COTTAGE, Meerhay Manor, Beaminster. 01308 862305. Converted two-bedroom barn for disabled.

Attractions

- FORDE ABBEY AND GARDENS, nr Chard. 01460 221290. Founded by Cistercian monks and built in 1148. The abbey is not accessible but it is still worth visiting because of the glorious gardens. Café, shop and disabled toilet. Buggy available and it is needed.
- MARINE AQUARIUM AND COBB HISTORY, The Cobb. 01297 443678. Accessible.

Shopping

The lower level around **The Cobb** is flat and there are tourist shops here. A very pleasant wheel/walk will take you into **Broad Street** – the main shopping street – but it is on a very fierce hill so take some strong help.

Eating and drinking

- HOLMBUSH, the main car park at the top of the hill, has a café and disabled toilets.
- THE HUNTERS LODGE INN, Charmouth Road 01297 33286. Large car park, one step to access.

Comment

Fascinating town which is unfortunately built on the side of a cliff. The harbour, esplanade and gardens, however, are accessible and there is level parking at either end of the esplanade.

The Purbecks: Swanage

In 876 the Danes were attacking King Alfred but as their fleet was on its way to Exeter it became overwhelmed in a storm and 120 tall ships were lost at **Studland Bay**.

Swanage is a pleasant, small, out of the way tourist resort with a nicely sheltered bay looking out towards the Isle of Wight. It is well known for its Purbeck stone, which has been used to build Westminster Abbey and many cathedrals throughout Britain and Europe.

John Mowlem, founder of the international construction company Mowlem, was born here in 1788. With his nephew, George Burt, he worked in London demolishing buildings, only to rebuild them in Swanage; look out for **Purbeck House** in the High Street as it is built with the chippings from the Albert Memorial.

Swanage tried to emulate the success of Weymouth in the early 1800s but it only really took off when the railway arrived.

Population

9,128

Accommodation

- MIDDLEBERE FARMHOUSE, Arne, nr Wareham. National Trust: 0845 4584422. Ground floor sofa bed, four first floor bedrooms. Adapted ground floor shower room and WC. www.nationaltrust.org.uk
- SANDYHOLME, Beach Road, Studland. 01929 450384. Ground floor flat. Ramped entrance. Twin bedroom, bathroom with bath lift.

- THE KNOLL HOUSE HOTEL. 01929 450450. Great position adjoining beach. Ground floor bedrooms but no adaptations. www.knollhouse.co.uk
- ISOLATION HOSPITAL, 2, Soldiers Lane, Corfe Castle. National Trust: 0845 4584422. Two miles from Corfe Castle. Three bedrooms. Adapted shower room and WC. Fantastic views. www.nationaltrust.org.uk
- DURDLE DOOR HOLIDAY PARK (seven miles west). 01929 400200. One wheelchair (ramp) accessible caravan. No other adaptations. www.lulworth.com

Attractions

- BLUE POOL, Furzebrook, nr Wareham. 01929 551408. Former clay pit. Set in 25 acres of gorse and heather. It's level but help is needed, as the path around the lake is sand. Free parking. Café and shop. Great disabled toilets!
- CORFE CASTLE (NT). Medieval royal fortress. Strong help needed. www.nationaltrust.org.uk
- LULWORTH COVE (five miles west). Important geological area. Very photogenic, lovely little creek. Concrete path from car park – moderate help needed. Disabled toilets. Accessible café and shop.
- TYNEHAM (four miles west). Fabulous forgotten village that was taken over by military for World War II preparation and never given back. Disabled toilets. *Recommended.*
- STUDLAND BEACH (NT) (two miles east). Knoll car park is accessible with boardwalks in the summer; also a specially designed wheelchair for the beach is available from Knoll visitor centre. www.nationaltrust.org.uk
- MGFT ANIMAL SANCTUARY, Church Knowle (three miles east). 01929 480474. Forgotten and abused animals.

- WAREHAM QUAY. Very pretty quay on banks of River Frome. Car park with disabled space. More for sitting and watching than wheeling into the sunset. Old Granary Restaurant is level but no facilities.
- MONKEY WORLD, Wool. 0800 456600. Everything you ever wanted to know about monkeys, lemurs etc. Moderate slopes but it can be managed by one person. Disabled parking. Two cafés. Disabled toilets. www.monkeyworld.org
- ARNE, nr Wareham. A nature reserve is hidden away here. It's the home of the rarely seen Dartford Warbler. The area is owned by the RSPB and National Trust – there are good walks/wheels to be enjoyed here.

Shopping

 There are no large towns in the Purbecks and the shopping is limited. Supermarkets are at Swanage Co-op, Pioneer and Somerfield. Wareham has Somerfield in the town with car park at the rear.

A farm shop at East Creech near Wareham has a range of fresh farm foods and deep frozen home made meals.

Eating and drinking

- WIMPY, 3 Institute Road, Swanage. 01929 422564. Step to enter.
- K'S EATING HOUSE, 1 Station Road Swanage. 01929 422396. Level access and disabled toilets.
- KEMPS COUNTRY HOUSE HOTEL, East Stoke, Wareham. 01929 462563. One step up into restaurant then level throughout but no disabled toilet. Excellent food.
- SPRINGFIELD COUNTRY HOUSE, Grange Road, Wareham. 01929 552177. 46 bedroom hotel, restaurant, health club, swimming pool. Ramps for entrance. No disabled toilet.

- ROSE MULLION, Wool. Opposite railway station. Small private car park. Toilets but no disabled.
- THE SEVEN STARS, East Burton. Accessible. Beer garden. Restaurant. No disabled toilet.

Comment

The Isle of Purbeck is stuck in a bit of a time warp – it hasn't caught up with the the 21st century yet.

Blandford Forum

A huge fire in 1731 destroyed the majority of the town. The subsequent rebuilding, with government and royal help, has left us with a fine example of a Georgian town and church. The unfortunately named Bastard brothers, William and John, designed and built the town. The name suggests Roman connections but there are none – it was a medieval scholar translating the name from Chipping Blandford and he got carried away. The main bulk of the town is accessible – especially **Market Place** – but help will be needed if a more detailed look is required.

Population

8,800

Parking

The main MARSH and HAM car parks will give access, via a small part covered shopping arcade, to Market Place.

Accommodation

- THE CROWN HOTEL, 8 West Street, Blandford. 01258 456626. Great position by the Stour. Level car park. One step into reception. Disabled toilets are on the first floor and there is a lift. The hotel is in the process of refurbishment and this will provide two en-suite bedrooms for wheelchair users.

Attraction

- BADBURY RINGS (NT), on the main A350 road to Wimborne. Important Iron Age site that the Romans used as a crossroad on their way to Old Sarum. www.nationaltrust.org.uk

Shopping

- TESCO superstore, Stour Park, Blandford. Disabled parking, café and disabled toilets.

Interesting individual shops off the main East Street but they are not that easy to enter.

Eating and drinking

- THE LANGTON ARMS, Tarrant Monkton, Blandford. Very attractive thatched pub, which you can arrive at through a ford. Good food. Level.

Comment

The Blackmoor Vale has many towns within it – Sherborne, Shaftesbury, Gillingham, Sturminster Newton, but Blandford has strong links with Poole, which is only 12 miles away and very popular with commuters.

Poole

Flints have been discovered which suggests a Bronze Age settlement here and a log boat dredged out of the harbour in the 1960s has been dated circa 395 BC. The Romans were here and occupied Hamworthy, naming it Moriconium. The nearby fortified town of **Wareham** was a stronghold of the West Saxons; it was also a target for the Danes. A great battle with the Danes and Alfred the Great took place in 876 with the Danes losing 120 ships off **Studland**. As Wareham's river approach silted up, Poole with its deeper channels became the popular choice.

In the 15th century a pirate character named Harry Paye was turned to by the authorities when they were under attack from the French. In the mid 15th century, Poole, like most of the ports on the south coast, enjoyed the rewards from the fishing around Newfoundland. Poole was the main town and the centre for trade with Newfoundland, and fortunes were made by the merchants of the town. The town was flourishing and by 1595 customs dues collected at Poole were over twice that of Bristol and Southampton.

In the 18th century Poole was entirely in the hands of its merchants who in turn brought Newfoundland and its government under their control. The town's population (5,000) depended on the merchants who were going through a very profitable period trading embargoed goods with Spanish and Portuguese towns blockaded by Napoleon. But it all changed after the defeat of Napoleon, resulting in bankruptcy for several merchants and ruin for the people of Poole.

The Industrial Revolution passed it by and steam ships, a cross-channel ferry and a railway arrived. Poole now was a supplier of Purbeck clay that was a vital ingredient for Wedgewood and Staffordshire potteries to produce bricks and pipes necessary for the building boom happening in Bournemouth. **Poole Pottery** was established, an ironworks was started to build locomotives and Marconi carried out his early wireless experiments from the Haven Hotel, Sandbanks, and from his yacht, *Elettra*. At the start of the 20th century Poole, with a population of just under 20,000, was in the shadow of its fashionable offspring Bournemouth.

Having learnt valuable lessons from the last century when it relied on just one source of wealth, the town set about attracting various industries to the town and from successful land deals including the release of **Canford Heath** for mixed residential and commercial development the borough was able to inject sufficient investment for infrastructure to provide for the town's future.

The result is a thriving and vibrant town that is flat and very accessible.

Population

133,050

Accommodation

- HOLES BAY BREWERS FAYRE PUB AND TRAVEL INN, Holes Bay Road, Poole. 01202 666994. Level car park and access to pub/restaurant and accommodation. Two en-suite bedrooms for disabled. www.travelinn.co.uk
- HOLIDAY INN EXPRESS, Walking Field Lane, Poole. 01202 649222. Disabled parking and one en-suite bedroom for disabled. www.hiexpress.com

- PREMIER LODGE, Technology Road, Poole. 0845 700 1538. Disabled parking and eight en-suite bedrooms for disabled. Accessible bar and restaurant. www.premierlodge.com
- DURLEY HALL HOTEL, Durley Chine Road, Poole. 01202 751000. Accessible building with lift and disabled toilet. No specific disabled bedrooms but larger family room used instead. Leisure suite with swimming pool. www.durleyhall.co.uk
- SANDFORD HOLIDAY PARK, Holton Heath, Poole. 0870 4422560. One fully accessible lodge sleeping six. Good on-site facilities including indoor and outdoor swimming pools, restaurant, shop, entertainment, take away and disabled toilets. www.westernstarholidays.co.uk
- ROCKLEY PARK HOLIDAY CENTRE, Rockley Park, Poole. 08457 753753. Two fully adapted caravans for disabled. On-site facilities include swimming pool, shop and bar. www.british-holidays.co.uk
- GREEN ISLAND HOLIDAY TRUST, Poole Harbour, Poole. 01202 740470. Swedish style log cabins designed for disabled.

Attractions

- BROWNSEA ISLAND (NT), Poole Harbour, Poole. 01202 797744. Haven for wildlife including red squirrels and many species of bird. Park at Poole Quay, all boats accept and help manual wheelchair users. Buggy (booking advised) is available and needed as there are some uneven surfaces and hills. Café and shop. Fantastic views. www.nationaltrust.org.uk/brownsea
- BOWLPLEX TENPIN BOWLING, 382 Poole Road, Branksome. 01202 765489. Parking. Accessible wheelchair lane. Café/restaurant.

- TOWER PARK ENTERTAINMENT, Mannings Heath, Poole. It looks functional and uninspiring but is actually one of the best entertainment venues in the south and is totally accessible. Free level car park with disabled spaces. Attractions include:
  - MEGABOWL, tenpin bowling. Lift to first floor. Wheelchair lift or two steps down to bowling lanes. Bar, Wimpy restaurant and pool table.
  - SPLASHDOWN, swimming pool. Several 'tubes'. Sitting area.
  - PIZZA HUT, accessible restaurant.
  - UCI MULTIPLEX, ten screen cinema. Snack bar. Spacious disabled toilets. No steps.
  - QUASAR, laser paint balling game in darkness (difficult in wheelchair!).
  - KFC, take-away. Accessible.
  - BURGER KING, restaurant and drive-thru take-away. Disabled toilets.
  - FRANKIE & BENNY'S bar and restaurant. Private car park. Accessible. Disabled toilets.
- POOLE PARK, Poole. This is one of Poole's main public attractions. Opened in 1890 by the Prince of Wales it is set very close to the town centre and only a couple of hundred metres from Dolphin Swimming pool. Disabled parking next to the lake. Just meandering alongside the lake in the gardens is very pleasant. For the more energetic there is crazy golf, tennis, bowls and rowing boats – for the less energetic there is a miniature railway that runs around the park. Disabled toilet. Café with further disabled toilets. Ice cream kiosks.
- POOLE POTTERY FACTORY OUTLET SHOP, The Quay, Poole. 01202 668681. Accessible with lift to first floor. Café. Disabled toilets for both sexes. www.poolepottery.co.uk

● COMPTON ACRES, Canford Cliffs Road, Poole. 01202 70077. Good access to all parts of this fascinating 12 acre garden representing different styles from around the world. Parking, shop and café. Disabled toilets. www.comptonacres.co.uk

● POOLE ARTS CENTRE, Poole. 01202 685222. Recently refitted and rebranded – now called LIGHTHOUSE. Parking in nearby public car parks. Setting down and picking up allowed. Various events throughout the year. Cinema, café, bar and theatre are all accessible. Lift and disabled toilets. www.pooleartscentre.co.uk

● SANDBANKS BEACH, Sandbanks. Good access. Poole Shopmobility 01202 661770 have 20 wide wheeled all-terrain wheelchairs for beach and sea access. Disabled toilets (RADAR).

● BRANKSOME CHINE. Car park with disabled spaces next to seafront. Possible to wheel/walk all the way to Bournemouth town centre. Café. Disabled toilet.

Shopping

● THE DOLPHIN SHOPPING CENTRE, Kingland Road, Poole. Excellent indoor shopping centre. Over 100 shops. Lift. Poole Shopmobility have their offices here 01202 661770. The centre is at the northern end of Poole High Street (pedestrianised) and it is possible to follow the route from the Dolphin Centre along the High Street through the pretty Old Poole area to the harbour. The High Street has a number of individual shops and national retailers.

Several out-of-town shopping centres including B&Q, Staples, Currys, PC World, Furniture Village, The Carphone Warehouse etc., and all are accessible.

Eating and drinking

- DARBY'S CORNER, 2 Waterloo Road, Broadstone, Poole. 01202 693780. Accessible pub. Level parking and disabled toilet.
- THE QUAY BREWSTERS, 21 The Quay, Poole. 01202 686050. Accessible. No car park. Disabled toilet.
- THE BAKERS ARMS, Lytchett Minster, four miles west. 01202 622900. Accessible Brewers Fayre Pub with level, gravelled car park. Disabled toilet.
- THE SHAH OF PERSIA, Longfleet Road, Poole. 01202 685346. Allocated parking. Ramped entrance. Disabled toilets.
- HARVESTER, Alder Road, Parkstone. (Next to Sainsbury's Talbot Heath). Disabled parking. Disabled toilet.
- FRANKIE & BENNY'S, Tower Park, Poole. Parking. Ramped entrance. Disabled toilets.
- YATES WINE LODGE, 89 High Street, Poole. 01202 683637. Excellent, spacious bar. Very comfortable and accessible. Good food – *recommended*. Disabled toilet.
- CYGNET CONTINENTAL CAFÉ, Poole Park. 01202 742842. Good level access. Disabled toilet (RADAR).
- BURGER KING, 134 High Street, Poole. Level access. Disabled toilet.
- McDONALD'S, 118 High Street, Poole. Level access but no disabled toilets.
- BEALES DEPARTMENT STORE, Dolphin Centre, Poole. Restaurant. Lift. Disabled toilets.

Comment

Poole is undoubtedly the place to visit. Good shopping, reasonable accommodation, entertainment, attractions, eating, drinking and they're all level! *Highly recommended.*

Bournemouth

Prior to 1810 Bournemouth did not exist. The River Bourne (no more than a stream) flowed to the sea through a gap in the crumbling cliff line. Captain Lewis Tregonwell was in charge of guarding the shoreline from **Hengistbury Head** to **Sandbanks**. His wife, Henrietta, a woman of considerable wealth fell in love with the place and they bought 8.5 acres of land for £179 and built a mansion for themselves (now part of the Royal Exeter Hotel). Smuggling was rife and Captain Tregonwell's involvement with the smugglers had been the subject of many rumours. The town is famous for the plantations of pine, which were started by Sir George Tapps in the early 19th century.

Without a harbour, trade for Bournemouth has always been a bit limited, having grown up in the shadow of its much older seafaring neighbour, Poole.

The arrival of the railway, as it has done for many towns, changed Bournemouth's fortunes. From a population of 6,000 in 1870 it shot up to around 60,000 by the end of the century. People were drawn to the pine-scented air, which was advertised as a cure to tuberculosis, and the physical beauty of the town also attracted more than its fair share of show business celebrities. Robert Louis Stevenson wrote Dr Jekyll and Mr Hyde while taking the TB cure here and Lillie Langtry, Edward VII's favourite mistress, has associations with the town.

There is fierce rivalry between Bournemouth and Poole. Poole has the harbour and **Branksome Park**, whilst Sandbanks, one of the worlds most expensive areas for residential property, is also a Poole address.

Bournemouth is the largest town in Dorset and is a hugely popular resort. Although known as a retirement area it has more nightclubs per square mile than anywhere else in the country after London.

Population

155,500

Accommodation

- THE CONNAUGHT HOTEL, West Hill Road, Bournemouth. 01202 298028. Close to the beach, disabled parking and disabled en-suite bedrooms. Lift. www.theconnaught.co.uk
- CARRINGTON HOUSE HOTEL, Knyverton Road, Bournemouth. 01202 369988. Disabled parking, ramped entrance and ground floor en-suite bedrooms. www.zoffanyhotels.co.uk
- BELVEDERE HOTEL, Bath Road, Bournemouth. 01202 293336. One double bedroom for disabled. Town centre. www.belvedere-hotel.co.uk
- DURLSTON COURT HOTEL, Gervis Road, East Cliff, Bournemouth. 01202 316316. One double bedroom for disabled. Lift and parking. www.seaviews.co.uk
- HEATHLANDS HOTEL, East Cliff, Bournemouth. 01202 553336. Adapted twin bedroom for disabled. Small step to enter. Parking. www.heathlandshotel.com
- NORFOLK ROYALE HOTEL, Richmond Hill, Bournemouth. 01202 551521. Central position. Parking. Ramp to entrance. Lift. Four twin bedrooms adapted for disabled. www.englishrosehotels.co.uk
- TRAVEL INN SMUGGLERS HAUNT, Rickets Cross, Ferndown, Bournemouth. 01202 874210. Next to

Smugglers Haunt Beefeater. Allocated parking. Two en-suite disabled bedrooms. www.travelinn.co.uk

Attractions

- ALICE IN WONDERLAND FAMILY PARK, nr Hurn Airport. 01202 483444. Mainly for younger children. Accessible.
- OCEANARIUM, Pier Approach, West Beach, Bournemouth. 01202 311993. Accessible attraction of marine life. www.oceanarium.co.uk
- VISTARAMA, Lower Gardens, Bournemouth. 01202 399939. Balloon flying trips. Concession for disabled.
- JET HERITAGE AVIATION MUSEUM, Hangar 600, Bournemouth Airport. Collection of restored vintage aircraft. Level parking and access.
- RUSSELL-COTES MUSEUM, East Cliff, Bournemouth. 01202 451800. Art gallery, museum, shop and café all recently re-furbished and all accessible. www.russell-cotes.bournemouth.gov.uk
- WALFORD MILL CRAFT CENTRE, Stone Lane, Wimborne, Dorset. 01202 841400. Contemporary craft and design. Different exhibition every month. Ground floor accessible with a few steps to mezzanine. Easy parking, disabled toilets, café/restaurant next door. www.walford-mill.co.uk
- STAPEHILL ABBEY GARDENS AND CRAFTS, 271 Wimborne Road, Wimborne, Dorset. 01202 861686. Cistercian abbey (first floor not accessible), garden centre, farmyard adventure playground, parking, coffee shop/restaurant and disabled toilets.
- MOORS VALLEY COUNTRY PARK, West Moors, Dorset. 01425 470721. Just off the A31 by Ashley Heath roundabout. 1,500 acres of forest, golf course, lakes and loads of footpaths – the majority of which are accessible. Disabled parking, café/restaurant, cycle

hire, visitor centre and disabled toilets. *Recommended.* www.eastdorset.gov.uk

- AVON HEATH COUNTRY PARK, Brocks Pine, St Leonards, Dorset. 01425 478470. The country parks are coming thick and fast now – this one is a short distance from MOORS VALLEY COUNTRY PARK. It has the feel of a motorway service station and the facilities and visitor centre are all a bit bleak but it is a Site of Special Scientific Interest and the walks/wheels are accessible.
- THE PAVILION THEATRE, Westover Road, Bournemouth. 01202 456400. Disabled parking for eight. Ramped entrance. Lift. Accessible toilets.
- BOURNEMOUTH PIER THEATRE, Bournemouth 01202 456400. The pier was built in 1855. Accessible. There is a new disabled toilet adjacent to the theatre and a second toilet near to pier entrance (ask staff for key).
- BOURNEMOUTH INTERNATIONAL CENTRE (BIC), Exeter Road, Bournemouth. 01202 456400. Vast entertainment/conference venue, swimming pool, fitness centre, bars and restaurant. Disabled toilets on all floors, lift and ramps. If approaching on foot/wheelchair from the town go past the stepped entrance and on the left is disabled access. By car, park on lower ground floor level where there are 12 allocated spaces. www.bic.co.uk
- ABC CINEMA, 27 Westover Road, Bournemouth. 01202 292612. Limited wheelchair access.
- ODEON CINEMA, Westover Road, Bournemouth. 01202 551086. Very limited access.
- IMAX 3D CINEMA, Pier Approach, Bournemouth. 01202 200000. After many false starts the cinema with a huge screen opened in 2002. Level access, lift and disabled toilets. www.bournemouthimax.com

Shopping

Bournemouth has a good selection of department stores and quality retail outlets but this is where the town's problems hit the wheelchair user as the hills are encountered. There are one or two disabled street parking places and it is a good idea to become acquainted with these.

- SOVEREIGN SHOPPING CENTRE, BOSCOMBE. Over 40 shops, two cafés and two disabled toilets. Boscombe Shopmobility 01202 399700.

Eating and drinking

- DEBENHAMS, The Square, Bournemouth. Café, lift, disabled toilets (RADAR).
- BEALES, 36 Old Christchurch Road, Bournemouth. Lift, café, two disabled toilets.
- BORDERS MUSIC AND STARBUCKS CAFÉ, The Square, Bournemouth. Very large bookshop and record store. Lift to first floor café and disabled toilets. *Recommended.*
- OBSCURA CAFÉ, The Square, Bournemouth. Eat in or outside. Level access. No disabled toilets.
- HARRY RAMSDEN, Pier Approach, Bournemouth. The fish and chip king has a great seafront position. Takeaway on beach level and sophisticated restaurant on first floor. All accessible and disabled toilet.
- UNCLE SAM'S AMERICAN DINER, 148 Old Christchurch Road, Bournemouth. Part accessible.
- THE TAP & HOBBIT, Bourne Avenue. 01202 290753. One shallow step to enter but the toilets are downstairs.
- ELEMENTS NIGHT CLUB, Fir Vale Road, Bournemouth. 01202 311187. Accessible, and ramp to toilets.

- BAR VIN, 165 Old Christchurch Road, Bournemouth. 01202 316664. Designed with disabled in mind. Ramped entrance and throughout. Disabled toilet.
- THE BRASSHOUSE, Westover Road, Bournemouth. 01202 314566. Accessible to all areas including coffee shop. Disabled toilet.
- THE LYNTON COURT, 47 Christchurch Road, Bournemouth. 01202 293992. Family pub/restaurant. Disabled toilet.

Comment

Thomas Hardy referred to Bournemouth as 'a Mediterranean lounging place on the English Channel' and I'm sure the residents of the town will see that as a glowing compliment. It is portrayed as a sophisticated, slightly upmarket resort and millions come here and enjoy their holiday every year, but it's not the most accessible town and a great deal is unavailable. This is not the town's fault – just nature and geology.

Christchurch

King Alfred fortified the town and the Normans built a castle. It was already a very important religious centre before the Normans arrived having 24 canons resident in the church. The church was demolished during the reign of William II and building of the massive parish church that stands here now began in 1094. During construction it was apparent a main beam had been cut too short. The builders left it one night and when they returned it was the correct length. After this 'miracle' the church was called 'Christ's Church' as He was, after all, a carpenter and thought to be responsible for stretching the beam. The name of the town was also changed from Twynham, which is what the Saxons called it, to Christchurch.

It is one of the most accessible towns in Dorset and a visit is definitely worthwhile.

Population

36,000

Accommodation

- BAILEY BRIDGE TRAVEL INN, next to Bailey Bridge Brewsters, Bailey Bridge, Barrack Road, Christchurch. 01202 485215. Two en-suite disabled bedrooms. Allocated parking. www.travelinn.co.uk
- SOMERFORD TRAVEL INN, next to Somerford Beefeater, Somerford Road, Christchurch. 01202 485376. www.travelinn.co.uk

Attractions

- MUDEFORD, Quay. Two miles from Christchurch at the harbour entrance. Mudeford is an enchanting place and an absolute must to visit. It is flat and the views from the esplanade are tremendous.
- BOAT TRIPS FROM MUDEFORD QUAY, Mudeford. 01425 272032. Wheelchair accessible catamaran.
- RED HOUSE MUSEUM, Quay Road, Christchurch. 01202 482860. Closed Mondays. Formerly a workhouse, the museum contains local and natural history artefacts, arts and crafts and a costume gallery.
- KNIGHTS OF CHRISTCHURCH, The Arena, 2 Riversmeet, Stoney Lane South, Christchurch. 01202 483777. Medieval jousts. Accessible. (Open May to September).
- CONVENT WALKS. Delightful walks/wheels around the Quomps and the convent walk. Great views of the Priory.
- THE PRIORY, Christchurch. The vast Priory dominates this part of the town. It is a very impressive structure and well worth a closer look – shame about all the handwritten 'please donate to our Priory' signs that proliferate inside.
- REGENT CINEMA, 51 High Street, Christchurch. 01202 479819. Several steps at front but there is a level side entrance – telephone first for arrangements. Chair lift but no toilets.

Shopping

Shopmobility have a branch here which is open on Mondays (Market day – accessible) telephone 01202 61770. The scooters are parked in the **Pioneer** supermarket car park.

Several small shopping arcades and the busy High Street selling all manner of goods.

Out of town shopping
- BAILEY BRIDGE SHOPPING CENTRE, Barrack Road. Comet, Petsmart, Carpet Depot, Halfords, Tempo are all here together with Pizza-Hut which is accessible and has disabled toilets.

Eating and drinking

- THE BOATHOUSE RESTAURANT, 6 Quay Road, Christchurch. 01202 480033. Great position adjoining and overlooking the Quomps and harbour. Accessible.
- PIZZA HUT, Barrack Road, Christchurch. 01202 490888. Ramp for access. Level inside and disabled toilets.
- BAILEY BRIDGE BREWSTERS PUB/RESTAURANT, Barrack Road, Christchurch. 01202 485215. Modern and very spacious pub and restaurant. Allocated parking. Disabled toilets.
- THE SOMERFORD BEEFEATER, Somerford Road, Christchurch. 01202485376. Level and accessible pub/restaurant. Disabled parking and disabled toilets.
- AVON CAUSEWAY HOTEL, Hurn. 01202 482714. Accessible. Disabled toilets.
- THE FAIRMILE, 202 Fairmile Road, Christchurch 01202 473499. Accessible. Disabled toilet.

Comment

Stuck on the far eastern side of the county, Christchurch has a lot to offer wheelchair users. The Quomps and the harbour are worth visiting and although it might seem like another suburb of Bournemouth the town has a distinctive character all of its own.

Devon

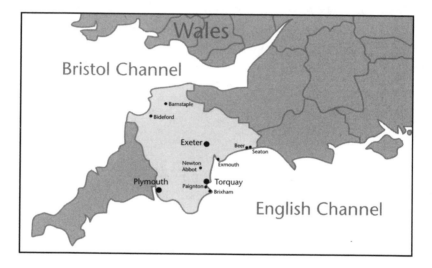

The history

Devon was the last part of Britain that the Saxons conquered, pushing the Dumnonii into Wales around 682. William the Conqueror came to Exeter in 1068 and was at first met with hostility, possibly because the mother of the defeated King Harold, Gytha, had already fled to Exeter with her daughter. But after negotiations they decided to let him in if he promised not to sack the town.

Devon was hit by the Black Death in the 14th century with a third of the population dying. During World War II, Plymouth was bombed out of all recognition. Slapton Sands was used by US forces for invasion trial run exercises in 1943 and Dartmouth became an important base for the invasion of Normandy a year later – an obelisk commemorating this stands at Slapton Sands.

The economy

Like all the counties in the West Country, Devon's average weekly pay is well below that of the rest of the UK. However, the unemployment rate of 2.6% is lower than the national average, whilst the rate of self-employment, at 15.6%, is higher than the national UK average (10.5%). Of course, what can't be factored into any equation is 'quality of life' but if it was, Devon with its clean air, ample open spaces, outstanding beaches and mild climate would undoubtedly rank very high.

In the past, the seafaring activities of Devonians resulted in major employment but now there is no dominant employer. Plymouth is the largest town with just over 250,000 people and it is still a major commercial and naval centre.

General

Devon has two coasts, 40 towns or villages and 12 or 13 rivers. It shares its borders with three other counties – Somerset, Dorset and Cornwall. Unlike Somerset and Dorset it has no Jurassic limestone and so has no refinement in its buildings. Devon whilst not a huge producer of tin, had many tin mines mostly on Dartmoor.

The Tamar forms the western boundary between Saxon Devon and Celtic Cornwall. King Athelstan made it the border in the tenth century and it has stayed that way just about ever since. Devon is the third largest county after Yorkshire and Lincolnshire and yet ranks only eighth in population terms for non-metropolitan counties – it is a sparsely populated county. The range of landscape varies from sub-tropical in the south to the harsh and unforgiving Dartmoor. The Romans, led by future emperor Vespasian, arrived here in AD49 and had many battles with the indigenous native Devonians called the Dumnonii. The Romans established themselves here but didn't venture much further west.

Dartmoor occupies the centre of the county – perhaps better for looking at rather than hiking through – but it truly is a beautiful and inspiring place.

North Devon is like an independent, self-contained county in its own right, having Barnstaple its capital, Ilfracombe and Westward Ho! the holiday resorts and Bideford the port trading with Wales and Ireland.

Barnstaple

Barnstaple (from Beardon Stapol) is an ancient town, granted its charter in 930 by King Athelstan. It is set at the head of the Taw and, until the estuary silted up in the 19th century, the town flourished as a port and the main market centre of North Devon. It still is the unrivalled capital of North Devon but its pre-eminence goes back further. In 1086 it was one of four Domesday boroughs in the county. Barnstaple's early prosperity was achieved through wool exports and later by importing Irish wool and yarn, which it then transported to factories elsewhere in the county. When the Taw silted up this trade was transferred to Bideford.

The golden years for Barnstaple were the 16th and 17th centuries when trade started up with America, but by the 18th century Bideford had overtaken it.

Population

25,412

Parking

- GREEN LANE SHOPPING CENTRE with disabled spaces on level 2A. Disabled toilets.
- NORTH WALK SHORT STAY car park is central and has disabled toilets.

Accommodation

- TRAVEL INN, Eastern Avenue, Whiddon Valley. Next to Barum Gate Brewers Fayre. 01271 377830. Two allocated parking spaces and en-suite bedrooms for disabled. www.travelinn.co.uk

- THE IMPERIAL HOTEL, Taw Vale Parade. 01271 324448. En-suite bedroom on first floor. Lift.
- CALVERT TRUST, Wistlandpound, Kentisbury. 01598 763221. Adventure holidays for disabled. Everything is accessible with all bedrooms en-suite. Heated indoor pool.
- LITTLE KNOWLE FARM, High Bickington, Umberleigh, Barnstaple. 01769 560503. Very attractive converted stone barns, one of which is adapted for wheelchair user. Well equipped gym.

Attractions

- ARLINGTON COURT (NT). 01271 850296. Neoclassical style, early 19th century house. Large collection of horse drawn carriages. Accessible gardens and buggy available. www.nationaltrust.org.uk
- MUSEUM OF NORTH DEVON, The Square. 01271 346747. Ground floor accessible and the first floor available via a Stannah lift. Disabled toilet.
- NORTH DEVON LEISURE CENTRE, Seven Brethern Bank. 01271 373361. Level parking, café, swimming pool hoist, and disabled toilets.
- ROCK PARK, adjacent to River Taw. Disabled toilets (RADAR).
- BRANNAMS POTTERY, Roundswell Industrial Estate. 01271 43035. A working pottery where you can try to produce your own work of art. Shop and restaurant.

Shopping

- SHOPMOBILITY, Albert Lane, Barnstaple. 01271 328866. It is located by the bus station and, as always, it is very well signposted. Shopmobility have their own private parking.

- GREEN LANES SHOPPING CENTRE. Situated at the heart of the town, squeezed in between Boutport Street and High Street. All shops (Dorothy Perkins, BHS, Principles, New Look, JJB Sports, Wimpy etc.) accessible. The centre also has its own wheelchair loan facility – to reserve please telephone 01271 322278. Disabled toilet (RADAR).
- THE HIGH STREET is partly pedestrianised and flat. Marks & Spencer, WH Smith, Boots and The Body Shop are here together with many individual private concerns. All the major banks are represented.
- ROUNDSWELL SHOPPING CENTRE includes:
  - SAINSBURY'S superstore. Disabled parking, café and disabled toilets.
  - SOMERFIELD, disabled toilets. MFI also has disabled toilets.
- WHIDDON VALLEY, St Johns Commercial Centre includes:
  - TESCO 24hr superstore. Level, allocated parking, café, and disabled toilet. Cash machines.
  - ST JOHN'S GARDEN CENTRE. Level and accessible.
  - LLOYDS PHARMACY, plus a veterinary clinic, a dental surgery, and a doctors' surgery.
  - WICKES BUILDING SUPPLIES, Homebase and a newsagent.
- PANNIER MARKET, High Street. Colourful 500 stall market operating six days a week. Well worth a look inside.

Eating and drinking

- MASSERELLA, Green Lanes Shopping Centre. Level access.
- WIMPY, 71 High Street. Level access and disabled toilets.

- THE OLD MEETING HOUSE, Green Lanes Shopping Centre. Level access.
- CHICAGO ROCK CAFÉ, Queens Street. Level access and disabled toilet.
- TESCO, Whiddon Valley. Disabled parking, café, and disabled toilets.
- McDONALD'S drive-thru and restaurant. Disabled parking and toilets.
- NORTH DEVON LEISURE CENTRE coffee shop and bar. Accessible.

Comment

Barnstaple, remember it's 'staple' not 'stable', is like a slightly smaller version of Taunton – it's functional rather than pretty. The town is fairly level and there is very good access all round – but it is not a shopper's delight.

Bideford

With the growth of trade to the New World in the 16th and 17th century Bideford became a very prosperous port and, even until the late 18th century, it was Devon's foremost port. Sitting on the west side of the **River Torridge**, this attractive town wins all the contests for looks and, although a lot of the town is built on a steeply climbing hill, it is a very pleasant place to spend some time. One of the reasons for the level access is that as the town expanded it did so on reclaimed land. Shipbuilding was carried out here until the 20th century. The quay is a delight! Visit it – you won't regret it and from here the town (the flat bit) can be explored.

Population

15,459

Accommodation/camping

- WESTWARD HO! BEACH HOLIDAY PARK, Westward Ho! 01271 866766. Adapted accessible bungalow with disabled toilets. www.jfhols.co.uk

Attractions

- RHS GARDEN ROSEMOOR, Great Torrington. 01805 624067. Forty-acre garden. Accessible. Disabled toilets in visitor centre.
- THE BIG SHEEP. Well signposted to the attraction. Very helpful staff. The car park is not that special but it is a fairly level access into the attraction. Patio restaurant and picnic area. Disabled toilet. Most features are accessible but the 'horse whispering' area needs

some improvement (the owner will be carrying this out shortly!). Dog trials, duck trials and Utopia Playground.

- BURTON ART GALLERY AND MUSEUM, Victoria Park. Accessible.

Shopping

The town is relatively level but the majority of shops are small independent operations and are not the most accessible.

- SAFEWAY superstore with disabled parking, café and toilets. Cash machine.
- ATLANTIC VILLAGE, Clovelly Road, off A39. 01237 422544. Covered shopping mall of about 30 shops. Several cafés border the open-air boulevard. The whole site is fully accessible. Cash machines. Disabled toilets. Children's play area is accessible. *Recommended.*
- BIDEFORD PANNIER COVERED MARKET, Market Hall. Ancient market in 19th century building having over 120 stalls and a small arcade of shops.

Eating and drinking

- WIMPY takeaway and restaurant. Disabled toilets.
- ATLANTIC VILLAGE, several cafés/restaurants. Either eat/drink in or out. Disabled toilets near.
- SAFEWAY café and disabled toilets.

Comment

A delightful small town providing an attractive alternative to Barnstaple's rather straightforward look. Lovely to spend some time in this classy place and the access is good.

Exmouth

Exmouth is the fourth largest town in Devon after Exeter, Torbay and Plymouth. Again, it is a nicely flat town and all its two miles or so of esplanade can be enjoyed. Its harbour lies just within the estuary, sheltered by **Exmouth Point**. As with so many seaside towns, by the mid-18th century, Exmouth was becoming a very popular place for people to bathe in the sea. The first houses built to overlook the sea were started in the late 18th century.

The town centre is pretty if not outstanding with new shops added over recent years. Most of the shops in the centre can be accessed but, as always, the most recently built are the best.

The **East Devon Coast** from Exmouth to Dorset has recently been ranked alongside the Great Barrier Reef and the Grand Canyon as one of the natural wonders of the world and the coast path starts here!

Population

30,980

Accommodation

- HOLBROOK FARM, Clyst Honiton, Exeter. 01392 367000. Well-proportioned rooms with wheelchair access. www.holbrookfarm.co.uk.
- DEVON CLIFFS HOLIDAY PARK, Sandy Bay, Exmouth. 01395 226226. Haven Holiday Park overlooking Sandy Bay and having a good range of facilities. Caravans adapted for disabled use.

Attractions

- CREALY ADVENTURE PARK, Sidmouth Road, Clyst St Mary, Exeter. 01395 233200. Theme park for young children. Allocated parking, ramps or level throughout but there are one or two nasty slopes. Three cafés, shop and disabled toilets. www.crealy.co.uk
- BICTON BOTANICAL GARDENS, East Budleigh Salterton. 01935 568465. Help will be needed as the gardens are on sloping ground. Car park but no allocated spaces, café, shop, disabled toilets. Miniature train takes customers around the park.
- OTTERTON MILL CENTRE, Otterton, Budleigh Salterton. 01395 568521. Water powered mill mentioned in Domesday Book. Charming craft centre. Parking. Café and shop together with bakery shop. No disabled toilets.
- STUART LINE CRUISES, Exmouth Marina. 01395 222144. Boat cruises. Accessible. www.stuartlinecruises.co.uk
- THE WORLD OF COUNTRY LIFE, Sandy Bay, Exmouth. 01395 274533. Large tourist attraction, which is accessible. www.worldofcountrylife.co.uk

Shopping

There is the usual range of shops for a mid-size town and seaside resort. The rebuilding of the new shopping centre helps to provide a reasonable range of retail units, the majority of which are accessible.

- TESCO 24hr superstore, Salterton Road, Exmouth. Petrol, café and toilets.
- DARTS FARM SHOPPING CENTRE, Topsham. 01392 875587. Organic and own grown produce, Gerald David butcher, Green Valley Cyder, Darts Farm

café, various shops, parking, accessible, disabled toilet. www.dartsfarm.co.uk

Eating and drinking

Cafés along the esplanade are accessible.

- THE DEER LEAP PUBLIC HOUSE, The Esplanade, Exmouth. Accessible.
- GOSSIPS CAFÉ, accessible but no disabled toilet.
- NO 5 THE GARDEN CAFÉ, 6–7 Fore Street, Topsham. Accessible.
- DARTS FARM CAFÉ, Darts Shopping Centre, Topsham. Fresh and very tasty food – best cooked breakfast anywhere!

Comment

Exmouth is good, it is fairly level and has good access and a pleasant 'open' feel to it.

Sidmouth

Another one of those towns that were merely a few fishermen's cottages until it was favoured with royal patronage. In 1819 the Duke and Duchess of Kent stayed with their infant daughter Victoria – later Queen Victoria. The town is set at the mouth of the **River Sid**. The town, however, did not expand quickly in the nineteenth century, unlike others, because the major landowners were not interested in development. Of course the 20th century saw an end to that, but expansion of the town has been carefully handled and the town still has a pleasant genteel air to it.

Population

13,606

Accommodation

- SALSTON MANOR HOTEL, Ottery St Mary, Exeter. 01404 815581. Six ground floor rooms suitable for wheelchairs and all public rooms accessible. www.salstonhotel.co.uk
- SID VALLEY COUNTRY HOTEL, Sidbury, Sidmouth. 01395 597274.
- LEMPRICE FARM, Yettington, Budleigh Salterton. 01395 567037. Quiet country position. One unit has accessible shower room.

Attractions

- DONKEY SANCTUARY, Slade House Farm, Sidmouth. 01395 578222. Founded in 1969 the sanctuary is a haven for mistreated or neglected donkeys.

It is the largest sanctuary for donkeys in the world. They operate 'riding therapy' for special needs children. The sanctuary is open every day and parking and entrance is free. Wheelchair access, café, shop and toilets. www.thedonkeysanctuary.org.uk

- NEWHALL EQUESTRIAN CENTRE, Killerton, Broadclyst. 01392 462453. Livery yard and equestrian centre. Small museum and exhibition of equestrian art. Accessible.
- KILLERTON (NT), Broadclyst. 01392 881345. Huge, 6,000 plus acre estate. Access is not bad but the ground slopes and there are a few steps to overcome. Restaurant and shop accessible. www.nationaltrust.org.uk
- WHEELING ALONG THE ESPLANADE. A major attraction for any seaside town come winter or summer is travelling up and down the promenade – the one at Sidmouth isn't that big so it doesn't tire you out.

Shopping

The main shopping street is fairly narrow but still a through road. Plenty of interesting shops here but access is not that good.

Comment

Charming seaside town that is accessible, although help needed to explore it all.

Seaton and Beer

Seaton was a busy fishing village until the mid-19th century. Then it was developed into a tourist resort by landowners the Trevelyans. Every year this pretty resort attracts numerous holidaymakers who come to the mile long pebble beach. The town has medieval links but there is little evidence of this.

Beer is a holiday and fishing village and goes with Seaton like fish and chips.

Population

8,372 (combined)

Accommodation

- LYME BAY HOLIDAY VILLAGE, 87 Harbour Road Seaton. 01297 626800. Chalets and apartments close to town centre. Many on-site facilities including swimming pool, games, café etc. www.lymebayholidayvillage.co.uk

Attractions

- PECORAMA, Beer. 01297 21542. Model railways and loads more. Accessible. www.peco-uk.com
- SEATON TRAMWAYS, Harbour Road, Seaton. Regular run to Colyton. Wheelchair users are easily accommodated.

Shopping

There is a weekly market (Monday).

A new Co-op general store has been built which has allocated disabled parking but no toilets.

Comment

A quiet seaside town that comes to life in the summer. It isn't too steep.

Exeter

The Romans arrived in Devon in AD50 and the Second Augustan Legion was stationed in Seaton in that year. A base was needed for a military headquarters for the South West of England and the Romans spied Exeter and got rid of the resident locals (the Dumnonii) and constructed their fortress. A symmetrically designed bathhouse was discovered during an excavation in the 1970s but unfortunately it is now hidden again. At the end of the 4th century most of the Romans had gone, recalled to fight the barbarians who were attacking Rome. This had a devastating effect on Exeter as the public buildings were not maintained and they slowly fell down. As we didn't seem able to govern ourselves it was left to the Saxons to show us the way and Exeter became part of the Kingdom of Wessex in 680. Our gallant leader Alfred became king in 871 and began to put the country in order and swept the Danes out of Exeter in 876. The Danes came back again in the 10th century with the sacking of Exeter in 1003.

In 1085 the Domesday Book was compiled which shows Devon had a population of around 60,000 with about 5,000 slaves.

Nowadays Exeter is a thriving and vibrant county town. The city centre is compact and level. The older parts blend easily with the modern redevelopments of shops and stores. Set in the middle of all of this is the cathedral. Its Norman twin towers and Gothic windows are all that survive from the mid 12th century when it was constructed.

Population

 94,717

Accommodation

 ● THE HOLIDAY INN EXPRESS, Exeter Business Park, Honiton Road. 01392 261000. Excellent lodge accommodation with good size en-suite shower room. Allocated disabled parking. The Barn Owl Pub is on the same site. www.hiexpress.com
● THE COUNTESS WEIR BEEFEATER, Topsham Road, Exeter. 01392 875441. Two disabled en-suite bedrooms for disabled. www.travelinn.co.uk

Attractions

 ● ROYAL ALBERT MEMORIAL MUSEUM AND ART GALLERY, Queen Street. 01392 665858. Set right in the middle of the city, this large museum has many displays and galleries. Ramped access and lift. Disabled toilets and parking for blue badge holders. www.exeter.gov.uk
● PHOENIX ART CENTRE, Gandy Street. 01392 667080. Level access next to Exeter Library. Ramped access at west side. Lift. Free parking for registered disabled – telephone for details.
● NORTHCOTT THEATRE, Stocker Road. 01392 493493. Ramped access via side entrance. Wheelchair accessible toilet.
● BARNFIELD THEATRE, Barnfield Road. 01392 271808. Ramped access available and disabled toilet but please ring first.
● EXETER CATHEDRAL, Cathedral Close. 01392 214219. One or two disabled parking spaces in close. Level access. Disabled toilet.

- POWDERHAM CASTLE, nr Exeter. 01623 890243. The farm shop and plant centre are accessible with wheelchair, the castle itself is limited. Disabled toilets.
- ODEON CINEMA, Sidwell Street, Exeter. 0870 5050007/01392 217175. Access is a bit of a fiddle and there is no disabled toilet although the toilet is wider than normal.
- PICTURE HOUSE, Bartholomew Street West, Exeter. 01392 430909. Fully wheelchair accessible to two-screen cinema.

Shopping

For a town of around 100,000 people it does have a splendid range of shops. This is because it serves a catchment area of over 250,000. The new shopping development (**The Guildhall Centre**) is very busy, and has a number of household names as tenants.

Eating and drinking

- THE TURKS HEAD, High Street, has an interesting history and was said to be frequented by Charles Dickens when he was reporting for the Morning Chronicle. The pub is accessible and there are disabled toilets. *Recommended.*
- THE REFECTORY, Exeter Cathedral, 1 The Cloisters. Great place for a coffee or lunch. Disabled toilets. Ramps to aid access.
- HOGSHEAD, 81–82 Fore Street. Accessible. Disabled toilets.
- BRAZZ, 10–12 Palace Gate, Exeter. Accessible. Disabled toilets.

There are many coffee shops here, ranging from small private concerns to large multi branch operations. Also, all the department stores have excellent cafeterias – the best being DEBENHAMS, although you cannot enjoy the view over the cathedral as that would entail going up two steps.

Comment

The city is similar in size to Bath and both hold many delights. Good road and rail links have helped Exeter to evolve into a charming and lively city, and thankfully an accessible one. It is one of the jewels of the south west and is definitely worth visiting.

Dartmouth

Situated close to Torbay nestling alongside the **River Dart**. The most dramatic way to enter Dartmouth is via the ferry at Kingswear. Waiting for the ferry to arrive you can see what must be one of the most picturesquely situated post offices in the UK, which has an outlook down the River Dart. From the ferry it is interesting to see the tier upon tier of streets of small houses along the hillside terraces – the waterside area is, like Bideford, built on reclaimed mudflats. In 1600 the muddy creek of **Mill Pool** was filled in to form what is now the **Market Square**, gardens and bandstand. Dartmouth originated from three riverside settlements, Clifton, South Town and Hardnesse. It is one of Devon's most ancient and attractive ports. Its sheltered position made it a favoured harbour from the early Middle Ages.

Between Land's End and the Isle of Wight there were only four deepwater ports that provided good anchorages for the fleet and were free from hazards. It was an assembly point for the large fleets on their way to the Holy Land in the Second and Third Crusades. In the 16th century Totnes merchants exported cloth and tin to France from here. Totnes later lost its status as a port to Dartmouth because of silting. Dartmouth is well known for its castle – built in the 14th century – that guards the mouth of the Dart, and the **Royal Naval College** that was built in 1905. Prior to this, trainee officers lived in ancient wooden hulks moored on the river.

Population

5,700

Accommodation

- THE OLD FORGE, Seymour Place, Totnes. 01803 862174. Small hotel near town centre. Step at front entrance. External level entrance to 'cottage suite' with spacious en-suite bathroom and shower.
- BEESON FARM, Kingsbridge. 01548 581270. Cottage designed for disabled amongst excellent converted farm buildings. Ground floor bedroom with en-suite roll-in shower and WC. www.beesonhols.co.uk

Attractions

- COLETON FISHACRE HOUSE AND GARDEN (NT), Kingswear, Dartmouth. 01803 752466. Designed in 1925 for Rupert and Lady Dorothy D'Oyly Carte. Lush gardens, gazebo and water features. A strong pusher will be needed. Disabled toilet. Ground floor only access to house. www.nationaltrust.org.uk
- WOODLANDS LEISURE PARK, Blackawton, Totnes. 01803 712598. Caravan park and tourist attraction – accessible and having disabled toilets. Many features, including huge indoor wet weather attraction. www.woodlandspark.com
- MARKET SQUARE has some very pleasant gardens with disabled toilets, and it's right by the main car park. Wheeling along the embankment is a delight and shouldn't be missed.

Shopping

Whilst the town centre is on level ground it is also ancient and has a number of cobbled streets.

Eating and drinking

- THE MARKET HOUSE INN has one step up for access.
- THE DOLPHIN, near car park, is accessible.

● THE STATION RESTAURANT, South Embankment, Dartmouth. Accessible, and enjoying outstanding views from its riverside position.

Comment

The local merchants back in the 14th century are to be thanked for reclaiming the land that Dartmouth occupies and making a level surface to wheel over. Because of the age of the buildings not much is accessible but it is still worth visiting.

Torbay

Torbay was an administrative creation in 1968 comprising the seaside resorts of Brixham, Paignton and Torquay. All three have distinctive characteristics.

Population

 115,582

Brixham

In medieval times the charming fishing port of Brixham was two places – Higher and Lower Brixham. The present harbour was built in the 18th century and the pier around 1800. This replaced the old harbour, which extended a lot further inland so as to give boats safe anchorage. In 1912 the breakwater was completed (work started in 1843). At the beginning of the 19th century Brixham was the major fish market in the West Country, it still is a busy, thriving port with many quayside stalls selling fresh fish. Beside the harbour there is a statue of William of Orange (William III) who landed here on 5 November 1688 on his way to take the throne from James II.

Population

See Torbay.

Accommodation

- HILLHEAD HOLIDAY CAMP, Brixham, Devon. 01803 853204. Panoramic views from this south-facing caravan site. Heated swimming pool, entertainment, bar, café etc. Wheelchair accessible.

Attractions

- BRIXHAM HERITAGE MUSEUM, Old Police Station, New Road. 01803 856267. Ground floor accessible museum. One step to enter. www.brixhamheritage.org.uk
- THE DEEP, Brixham Quay. Stories from the ocean, animated pirates – good fun for kids. Ground floor.

- BERRY HEAD. This is a small country park occupying the headland at Berry Head. A Napoleonic fort juts out into the sea and there are pleasant wheels/walks to be enjoyed here – some unevenness with the paths. Accessible toilets.
- BRIXHAM AQUARIUM, The Quay. 01803 882204. Level access.
- BRIXHAM THEATRE. Accessible. Lift.

Shopping

 Brixham isn't very big with just one street offering shopping facilities including a Co-op in Fore Street, which has level access and wide aisles.

Eating and drinking

 There are accessible cafés around the quay.

- THE BERRY HEAD HOTEL, Brixham. 01803 853225. Accessible restaurant but no disabled toilets.
- VIGILANCE, 4 Bolton Street. 01803 850489. Level and disabled toilet.
- SPINNAKER RESTAURANT, Brixham Marina. 01803 852121. Level access. Some amendments to toilet.

Comment

Park at Freshwater Car Park and wheel into the centre – fantastic views. (Shopmobility, Central Park 01803 858304.)

Paignton

Prior to the Reformation, Paignton was one of the richest manors of the Bishop of Exeter. In fact Paignton was once the largest settlement in Torbay. It flourished in the 16th and 17th centuries but by 1800 that had all fallen away. Victorian engineers built a seawall that gradually enabled land to be reclaimed, which has produced a great, level area just right for wheelchairs!

Paignton Pier was built in 1878 when the only building was a pavilion sat on the very end that was the height of Victorian sophistication. It now looks a bit unkempt – but at least it's still there. Now Paignton has been swallowed up by Torquay and has lost some of its individuality.

Population

See Torbay.

Accommodation

See Torquay.

Attractions

- PAIGNTON ZOO, Totnes Road, Paignton. 01803 697500. Over £6,000,000 has been spent on the zoo and environmental park and it is accessible. At over 75 acres, it is also one of this country's largest and best. Parking, restaurant, takeaway, and disabled toilets. Make sure a strong pusher is with you as there are a number of inclines throughout the zoo. www.paigntonzoo.org.uk

- APOLLO CINEMA, Esplanade, Paignton. 01803 555577. Nine screen cinema. Disabled parking spaces. Disabled toilets. Lowered box office. Wheelchair access.
- PALACE THEATRE, Palace Avenue. 01803 665800. Chair lift, accessible toilet. Limited space for wheelchair, please telephone first.
- PAIGNTON SANDS, accessible. Accessible toilets.

Shopping

 A good range of shops are available at Paignton and it is all level.

- SHOPMOBILITY, Victoria Car Park, Garfield Road. 01803 521771.
- TESCO, Victoria Street. Level access.
- SAINSBURY'S, Brixham Road. Parking. Accessible toilets.
- SAFEWAY, Totnes Road. Parking, level access, disabled toilet.

Eating and drinking

- PRIORY TOWERS, 21 The Esplanade. Level access.
- INN ON THE QUAY BREWERS FAYRE, Tanners Road, Goodrington. 01803 559754. Level access. Disabled toilets.
- TALK OF THE TOWN, Torbay Road. Level access and accessible toilets.

Torquay

At 35,000 BC the oldest remains in the county, if not the whole country, have been found at **Kents Cavern** (many of the relics are on display in the Torquay museum). The next historical piece to note was the founding of **Torre Abbey** in 1196 as a monastery. The land was given by William de Brewer who in turn was gifted the land by Richard the Lionheart as a thank you for William's son helping in his release from Austria. After the dissolution of the monasteries in 1539 the abbey was modified into a private residence and later purchased by the Cary family. Apart from that there isn't a huge amount of history to Torquay until the end of the 18th century when development as a seaside resort started. The south coast of Devon began to be exploited for the new fashion of sea bathing and Torquay's special asset of a mild climate was particularly in demand for consumptive invalids, including Elizabeth Barrett Browning who spent three years here. The 19th century charm has gone but it has been replaced by a brasher, more colourful, flatter and more accessible town centre. Agatha Christie was born and lived here. She is remembered with many tributes to her throughout the town.

Population

See Torbay.

Accommodation

All towns have little in the way of accessible accommodation but a major seaside resort such as Torquay should have some accessible hotels.

- JOHN GROOMS HOLIDAY FLAT, 1 Park Road, Babbacombe, Torquay. 01446 771311. Fully adapted ground floor flat with double bedroom, electric hoist and shower. Two sofabeds in lounge.
- THE CORBYN SELF CONTAINED FLATS, Torbay Road. 01803 215595.
- FRAGNEL HALL HOTEL, Higher Woodfield Road, Torquay. 01803 298339. Level car park. Lift. Dining room accessible. No specific facilities. www.frognellhall.co.uk

Attractions

- KENTS CAVERN, Ilsham Road, Torquay. 01803 215136. Concrete paths throughout but there are seven steps. Strong help needed. Free car park. www.kents-cavern.co.uk
- BABBACOMBE MODEL VILLAGE, Hampton Avenue, Torquay. 01803 328669. Fit help needed as most of attraction is set on hill. www.babbacombemodelvillage.co.uk
- OVERBECKS MUSEUM AND GARDEN (NT), Sharpitor, Salcombe. 01548 842893. Ground floor of house only accessible. Shop and tea room accessible. The garden is steep so strong help needed. www.nationaltrust.org.uk
- AMF BOWLING, Torwood Street. Accessible throughout and bowling lane for wheelchair user.
- RIVIERA CENTRE, Torquay. Modern entertainments and conference venue. Parking. Swimming pool with wave machine. Ice rink. Accessible disabled toilets.
- COCKINGTON MANOR, Torquay. Heritage/time warp village. Horse drawn trips. Level. Good place for a picnic.

- TORRE ABBEY, Kings Drive, Torquay. 01803 293593. The house is not accessible but the ruins and gardens are. www.torre-abbey.org.uk
- CENTRAL CINEMA, Abbey Road. 01803 380001.
- PRINCESS THEATRE, Torbay Road. 0870 2414120. Separate entrance for wheelchairs. Accessible bar. Please telephone first.
- BABBACOMBE THEATRE, Babbacombe Downs Road. 01803 328385. Space for two wheelchairs, telephone first please.

Shopping

 Torquay has some excellent shops and the majority are accessible without the need of a strong helper! The area around the harbour is perfect for spending a few hours looking around the shops – Debenhams department store is located on **The Strand** and the very impressive new shopping complex is along **Fleet Street**. This is where you can find designer goods in very pleasant and elegant surroundings. There is Laura Ashley and Laura Ashley 'Clearance Furniture Outlet', T.K. Maxx, The Body Shop, WH Smith etc. Around the harbour are more seasonal shops and the usual cafés, takeaways and pubs.

Beside the pier is **The Pavilions Shopping Centre**, which provides more accessible shopping, is level to enter (lift to first floor) and has a disabled toilet.

Travelling further into the town along **Fore Street** (moderate slope at first) you will come across other shops including another WH Smith, Next, Argos, an accessible Post Office and a small shopping centre (**Union Square**) which houses, amongst others, Somerfield supermarket. The road gets steeper and help will be needed as you travel away from the harbour and beach.

Out of town shopping
Two or three miles out of Torquay heading towards Exeter you'll find a modern shopping complex. Shops include Staples, Sainsbury's and a McDonald's drive-thru takeaway and restaurant.

Eating and drinking

 There's a large number of cafés in town including KFC, Burger King with disabled toilets, McDonald's level with disabled toilets, Pizza Express, Loggerheads (*recommended*), and Shauls (Union Square) which is accessible and serves good coffee.

- CAFÉ PRAGUE, Castle Circus. 01803 293000. It's quite a climb from the harbour side.

Pubs
- HOGSHEAD, 3 Union Street (accessible to ground floor only). 01803 219550.
- CAFÉ BAR MOJO,Torbay Road. 01803 294882.
- YATES, Fleet Street. Accessible.
- LONDON INN, 15 The Strand. 01803 380003. One step to enter. Stair lift to all floors. Disabled toilets (RADAR).
- VAUGHANS WINE BAR, 3 Vaughan Parade. 01803 290922.
- CRAZY HORSE SALOON, Harbourside. Accessible.

Comment

It is said to be sad and garish and with a good future behind it. A forgotten town trying desperately to re-live its heydays. Actually it isn't any of these – it is a superb, friendly place that provides some of the most thoughtful and accessible places to visit, shop and enjoy oneself in. Torquay is one of the best and I would urge anyone to visit it – you won't be disappointed.

Plymouth

Plymouth lies between the rivers Plym and Tamar at the entrance to the English Channel and has one of the finest natural harbours in the world. Stone Age people lived on the northern shore of the Plym estuary about 20,000 years ago. Plymouth started to become established when the Saxons were here. They developed a small fishing village at the mouth of the Plym and called it Sudtone (South Farm).

The silting up of the River Plym left Plympton losing its trade to Sutton (Sudtone) and Sutton's fortunes changed from an unimportant fishing village into an international trading port. By the 14th century Sutton became Plymouth.

In 1337 Sutton Pool was given to the Duchy of Cornwall by Edward III – it was later sold for £38,000 to the Sutton Harbour Company in 1891. Nowadays it has lost its scruffy and broken down look and has been transformed into a vibrant commercial centre again, but this time for shops, pubs and restaurants.

Plymouth began to expand as a shipbuilding town in the 15th century with many large ships built in the **Plymouth Sound.**

When talking of Plymouth two major historical connections spring to mind. First there is Francis Drake who was born in 1543 (exact date unknown) in a two room cottage on the banks of the River Tamar: the family lived in one room and their farm beasts lived in the other. They moved to the east coast of England and lived in the hulk of a ship. They were very poor and, to escape the poverty, it wasn't long before young Francis Drake joined his cousin John Hawkins on many seafaring adventures i.e piracy. For these exploits he was due to be hanged but Queen Elizabeth I found he had his uses. He actually brought back more money than was in the whole of the English exchequer!

In 1572 he attacked Spanish ships in the Caribbean but was badly wounded. After recovering he landed at Panama, plundered a bullion convoy and continued across the Isthmus where he saw the Pacific Ocean – the first Englishman to do so. Between 1577 and 1580 he circumnavigated the world on board the *Golden Hind*. He was knighted on his return and gave his investors a huge 4,700% return on their investment.

In 1585 he married Elizabeth Sydenham, an heiress from Somerset, and they purchased **Buckland Abbey** from Drake's rival, Sir Richard Grenville. He then helped the English fleet to defeat the Spanish Armada in 1588. He became Lord Mayor of Plymouth and its MP. In 1596 Drake left with Hawkins for another 'adventure', this time to Panama, but it resulted in both of their deaths – Drake's from dysentery. He was buried at sea in a lead coffin. It's quite a story: poverty to great wealth, insignificance to a knighthood, hovel to mansion; zero to hero!

The other famous event was in 1620 when the Pilgrim Fathers sailed to Plymouth, Massachusetts (a coincidence and not named by them) in the *Mayflower* – a ship no bigger than two buses. The puritanical movement had started about 40 years earlier in Nottingham. When members found themselves the subject of persecution they looked elsewhere to live their simple and godly way of life. They first went to Holland but after 12 years, and with worries about losing their mother tongue, they decided to go to America. James I gave them permission to establish a settlement in the New World.

Virginia was the intended destination but they got blown off course. Some of the Pilgrim Fathers and crew stayed their last night in England at **Island House** that is now the Tourist Information Centre.

There are 43 other Plymouths around the world with 30 in the USA alone.

World War II shaped the town more than any other event in its long history. The town centre was flattened but the Barbican was somehow saved.

Population

243,895

Accommodation

- NOVOTEL, Marsh Mills, Plymouth. 01752 221422. Pleasant and very comfortable hotel on the edge of the city. Accessible. Disabled parking. Two bedrooms with en-suite bath/shower for disabled. Level throughout. Outdoor pool. Novotel is a French company and it does have a certain Gallic flair – especially with the food! www.novotel.com
- COPTHORNE HOTEL, Armada Way, Plymouth. 01752 224161. Quality hotel over several levels. Lifts but not to basement parking. When inside it's all very accessible – but it's getting in that's the problem. One bedroom (out of 135) adapted for disabled guests. Leisure suite with pool and gym.
- ASTOR HALL, 157 Devonport Road, Plymouth. 01752 562729. Owned by Plymouth & District Disabled Fellowship, providing 24-hour care. Respite and holidays. www.astorhall.co.uk
- IBIS HOTELS, Longbridge Road, Marsh Mills, Plymouth 01752 601087. This is owned by the same French group who have the nearby Novotel. Spacious and level rooms. Two bedrooms with disabled bathrooms. Lodge accommodation. www.accorhotels.com

- NEW CONTINENTAL HOTEL, Millbay Road, Plymouth. 01752 220782. Accessible. www.newcontinental.co.uk
- LOCKYERS QUAY BREWERS FAYRE, Travel Inn, Coxside, Plymouth. 01752 254180. Centrally sited accommodation next to very pleasant and very comfortable Brewers Fayre pub that is level throughout and has disabled toilets. Two en-suite bedrooms for disabled guests. www.travelinn.co.uk
- MARSH MILLS BEEFEATER, 300 Plymouth Road, Plymouth. 01752 600660. Another hotel around Marsh Mills roundabout. Two en-suite bedrooms for disabled. www.travelinn.co.uk
- TRAVELODGE, Saltash. 08700 850950. Located just over the Tamar and into Cornwall. Next to Little Chef. Two en-suite bedrooms with disabled bathrooms. www.travelodge.co.uk
- OSMOND GUEST HOUSE, 42 Pier Street, Plymouth. 01752 229705. Limited access. Two ground floor en-suite bedrooms. Central. www.plymouth-explore.co.uk
- MOUNT BATTEN CENTRE, 70 Lawrence Road, Mount Batten. 01752 404567. The centre provides simple accommodation either for overnight or longer. Set up for able bodied and disabled. Lifts give access throughout. En-suite and breakfast if required. www.mount-batten-centre.com

Attractions

- NATIONAL MARINE AQUARIUM, Rope Walk, Coxside, Plymouth. 01752 600301. New and very impressive attraction, highlighting Plymouth's association with the sea, fishing and fish. Excellent facilities for wheelchair users. Parking. Café. Disabled toilets. www.national-aquarium.co.uk

- MORWELLHAM QUAY, Morwellham, Tavistock. 01822 832766. Accessible, recreated Victorian port and mine. Disabled toilets. www.morwellham-quay.co.uk
- ANTONY HOUSE (NT), Torpoint, Plymouth. 01752 812191. Early 18th century manor house. Ground floor of house accessible plus stairclimber for upper floors. Gardens accessible. Shop and café accessible. www.nationaltrust.org.uk
- BUCKLAND ABBEY (NT), Yelverton. 01822 853607. Originally a Cistercian abbey, but better known as the home of Sir Francis Drake. Exclusive parking close to house. Volunteer-driven buggy. Awkward steep site. Help needed to see more than just the shop and vegetable garden. Disabled toilets. www.nationaltrust.org.uk
- SALTRAM (NT), Plympton, Plymouth. 01752 333500. George II mansion and 18th century gardens. House accessible, lift to first floor. Gardens, shop and tearooms accessible. www.nationaltrust.org.uk
- PLYMOUTH PAVILIONS, Millbay Road, Plymouth. 01752 222200. Entertainments venue, swimming pool with wave machine, ice rink, stage/arena, restaurant and disabled toilets. Level access to most parts but ring first. www.plymouthpavilions.com
- THEATRE ROYAL. 01752 267222. Very good facilities for wheelchair users. Lower counters at box office and coffee bar, lift to all floors and they even bring drinks to you in the intermission. Disabled toilets. www.theatreroyal.com
- PLYMOUTH DOME, The Hoe, Plymouth. 01752 603300. Recreated Elizabethan Street, a journey through 400 years of local history, including the voyages of Drake, Cook and the Pilgrim and the devastation of the Blitz. Accessible
- BARBICAN GLASSWORKS, The Old Fish Market, The Barbican. 01752 224777. Dartington Crystal

own this attraction and it includes glassblowing demonstrations. The shop is in a great position on the water's edge.

- PLYMOUTH MAYFLOWER The Barbican Quay, Plymouth. 01752 306330. Fascinating, interactive new multi-million pound attraction telling the story of Plymouth. Fully accessible. Disabled toilets. www.plymouth-mayflower.co.uk
- PLYMOUTH MUSEUM AND ART GALLERY, Drake Circus, Plymouth. 01752 304774. Level access to museum via side entrance. Lift to upper floors. www.ply mouthmuseum.gov.uk
- MOUNT BATTEN CENTRE, Lawrence Road, Mount Batten, Plymouth. 01752 404567. All things to do with water sports. The centre is wheelchair friendly with café, bar and disabled toilets. Water taxi. www.mount-batten-centre.com
- ABC CINEMA, Derrys Cross, Plymouth. 01752 225553. The largest screens in Plymouth! Disabled access. www.abccinemas.co.uk
- WARNER VILLAGE, Barbican Leisure Park, Shapsters Road, Coxside, Plymouth. 01752 670084. Over 3,000 seats and 15 screen cinema. Parking. Disabled access and disabled toilets. Also on the same site are restaurants, bars, nightclubs, superbowl and leisure centre. www.warnervillage.co.uk

Shopping

 The town is well blessed with a huge variety of shops. The majority are accessible. Department stores such as Derrys have made a big effort to make their store as accessible as they can with a level access at the rear (New George Street) that leads to the lifts. Individual shops and indoor markets are all around the town centre area. Department stores such as Debenhams and Dingles,

Littlewoods and Marks & Spencer are all in this area and it is flat. **The Barbican** has ancient cobbled streets and is hard work, very few of the shops are fully accessible apart from **Dartington's Glass Works** which is totally accessible. The Barbican has a number of interesting individual shops and galleries including Beryl Cook's shop. To access all of the shopping and the Barbican, telephone Shopmobility 01752 600637 who have their own car park at **Mayflower East Car Park** – follow the signs.

Eating and drinking

- HOBBS CHOCOLATE AND COFFEE HOUSE. 34 Mayflower Street, Plymouth. 01752 667843. Accessible ground floor seating.
- DEBENHAMS, Royal Parade, Plymouth. 01752 266666. Accessible restaurant and Venue coffee shop.
- DERRYS, New George Street. Lift access to café/ restaurant. Plenty of room to park buggy.
- BAR ZEGG CO., 4 Frankfurt Gate, Plymouth. 01752 664754. One step, but level after. www.zeegco.com
- THE EAGLE, Cornwall Street. Accessible pub in city centre.
- GOG AND MAGOG, (Weatherspoons) bar situated in The Barbican. Concrete ramps for access. Accessible and disabled toilets.
- CARWARDINES COFFEE SHOP AND CAFÉ, accessible.
- OGGY OGGY PASTY CO., café, accessible.
- PIZZA & PASTA, one step into restaurant.
- HOGSHEAD, 12–14 Royal Parade, Plymouth. 01752 260442. Accessible.
- YATES WINE LODGE, 28 Royal Parade, Plymouth. 01752 257884. Accessible.
- FIRKIN DOG HOUSE, 174 Union Street, Plymouth. 01752 253226. Accessible.

Comment

A bit of a disappointment. By far the largest town in the West Country, but it lacks facilities for disabled that are found in much smaller towns. The new facilities now being constructed are redressing the balance a little, but there is no hotel in the centre that provides disabled rooms with en-suite shower/bathrooms. It might boast a five star hotel or two but even they don't have the necessary facilities.

Newton Abbot

Founded alongside **Torre Abbey** not long after the abbey itself was founded in 1196. Newton Abbot began as two towns at the head of the Teign Valley – Newton Abbot and Newton Bushel occupied opposite sides of the River Lemon.

A market town since 1220, Newton Abbot is an excellent place to visit and/or stay because the town is so flat. It's not an obvious tourist haunt but it is a busy and thriving town and a good starting point to visit **Dartmoor.**

Population

25,212

Accommodation

● WOODER MANOR, Widecombe-in-the-Moor, Newton Abbot 01364 621391. Two accessible self-catering farm cottages (out of six). Working Dartmoor farm.

Attractions

● STOVER COUNTRY PARK, Newton Abbot. Haven for birds and wildlife. Walks/wheels around lake. Visitor/information centre. Car park. All accessible.
● GORSE BLOSSOM MINIATURE RAILWAY AND WOODLAND PARK, Bickington, Newton Abbot. 01626 821361.
● BRADLEY (NT), Newton Abbot. 01625 354513. Small medieval manor. House ground floor and gardens accessible. www.nationaltrust.org.uk

- THE CHURCH HOUSE (NT), Widecombe-in-the-Moor, Newton Abbot. 01364 621321. Ground floor accessible. www.nationaltrust.org.uk
- HEDGEHOG HOSPITAL, Denbury Road, Newton Abbot. 01626 362319. All parts of farm accessible although bumpy in places. Disabled toilet. www.hegdehog.org.uk
- NEWTON ABBOT RACECOURSE, Newton Abbot. 01626 353235. National Hunt racing during the winter months and various events during the summer including regular stock car racing. Accessible and lift to upper floors.
- LA BOWL, tenpin bowling. Accessible and with parking.
- TRAGO MILLS, shopping and leisure centre, nr Stover, Newton Abbot. 01626 821111. Shopping, golf, children's amusements, cafés and take away. This was Trago Mills first outlet. Accessible.

Shopping

Newton Abbot has an extensive range of shops – The Body Shop, New Look, Somerfield supermarket, WH Smith are all represented. **The Market Walk** shopping centre is level and there are disabled toilets at the entrance. The indoor market has a good range of stalls including butchers, bakers etc. The shopping precinct and the main shopping street (Queen Street) are level. Shopmobility are in the multi-storey (Market) car park 01626 335775. Out of town shopping includes Tesco 24hr superstore with parking, café and disabled toilets. Tesco petrol station with 'fast card'.

Eating and drinking

- 3 COOKS CAFÉ & SHOP, Queen Street, Newton Abbot. Level access.

- THE OFFICE, 13 Queens Street, Newton Abbot. 01626 354238. Accessible pub. One step to enter.
- COURTENAY ARMS, 45 Queen Street, Newton Abbot. 01626 351695. Accessible.
- THE CHICKEN CAFÉ, First Floor (accessible from multi-storey car park), Market Walk Shopping Centre, Newton Abbot.
- BURGER KING, Queen Street, Newton Abbot.
- WIMPY, Queen Street, Newton Abbot.
- RICHARD HOPKINS, a Wetherspoon pub, Queen Street, Newton Abbot. 01626 323930. Spacious, refurbished town centre pub, which has level access. Main bar area is level and has smoking/non smoking areas. Disabled WC.
- McDONALD'S DRIVE-THRU AND RESTAURANT, parking and disabled toilets.

Comment

Newton Abbot is an impressive and straightforward town. It also offers tremendous access for a wheelchair user. Some of the shops in Queen Street are still difficult to enter but generally it is one of the better towns visited.

Cornwall

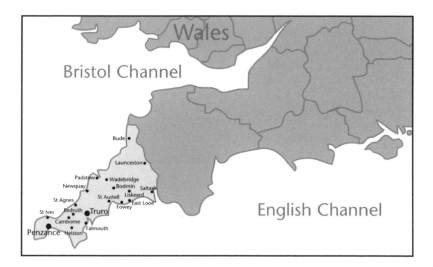

The history

It is thought that in the Early Stone Age the first holi-daymaker arrived in Cornwall (The Emit – Cornish for holiday visitor) but they didn't settle here until the Middle Stone Age (10,000 BC). The settlements were around The Lizard and Bodmin Moor.

The New Stone Age (4,000–2,400 BC) and neolithic man was fortifying his Carn Brea settlement and introducing the first Cornish hedges. Early Bronze Age (2,400–1,500 BC) and Cornwall started to use its major resources of tin and copper. It is reckoned that the Celts arrived around this time.

In 8 BC Cornwall was named *Belerion* – The Shining Land – by Diodorus Siclusthis, it was the first place to be named in Britain for geographical reasons.

The Roman invasion didn't extend into Cornwall, but English merchants came to trade with the Romans. After the Romans left, England was a pagan country but not so in Cornwall where Christianity continued to grow with many parish churches named after Celtic saints. The first Christian church in Britain is St Piran's Oratory built in the 6th century.

In 936 King Athelstan fixed the east bank of the Tamar as the boundary between Anglo-Saxon Wessex and Celtic Cornwall.

Until the mid-1300s Cornish was widely spoken, but the Celtic language, which is closely related to Welsh, all but died out as English spread, and when in 1547 Edward VI instructed that the *Book of Common Prayer* be introduced and that Celtic customs be discontinued it effectively ended the language. Having said that, plans for a revival were set up almost immediately and now it is believed that there are some 3,500 Cornish speakers. The language is officially recognised by the government and will be classed as a minority language and given legal protection under European law.

In the 14th and 15th centuries valuable metals were found underground but it was not until the 18th and 19th centuries that more powerful steam engines were built to enable deep mining and this brought huge prosperity to Cornwall.

In 1746 William Cookworthy discovered china clay near Helston and soon afterwards he found larger deposits at St Stephen, which effectively led to the china clay industry in the county.

By the mid-19th century Cornwall's economy was booming. It was the world's leading copper ore producer and their mining and engineering expertise was in demand all over the world, which led to mass emigration to Africa, Mexico, Australia, Canada and the USA. By 1863 there were 63 miles of underground workings and the mines employed 2000 people. But in 1866 disaster struck as copper prices collapsed and the de-industrialisation of Cornwall began.

In 1834 Scilly became the first place in Britain to have compulsory education.

In 1890 Bob Fitzsimmons of Helston became the first native Briton to win the world heavyweight boxing championship – he also won three other world titles. In 1901 Marconi sent the first transatlantic radio signal from Cornwall.

On March 18, 1967, the Torrey Canyon disaster occurred – nearly 120,000 tons of crude oil was spilled and the entire Cornish coastline, north and south, was polluted.

In 1999 Cornwall was awarded Objective 1 status and, in an effort to stop young people leaving the county, a new university was planned, with its main campus at Falmouth.

Famous people from Cornwall's past include in the 19th century Humphry Davy who discovered chlorine as a bleaching agent and produced the miners' safety lamp, Andrew Pears, from Mevagissey, who perfected the process of refining soap, Richard Lander who discovered the source of the River Niger and Robert Hawker who introduced the harvest festival, a former pagan celebration.

The economy

Cornwall is one of the United Kingdom's fastest growing counties with the fourth largest population growth of any shire county. Over the last 20 years the population has grown by 17.5% against a UK average growth rate of 4.3%. Inclusive of the Isles of Scilly the total figure now stands at 501,300.

However, the resident population is dwarfed by the four million or so tourists (the return of the emit!) that Cornwall attracts every year. They are drawn to the beautiful scenery and stunning coastline.

But Cornwall is a deprived region. Wages are only 78% of the UK average and unemployment, unlike the rest of the country, is rising.

General

So those are the facts, but what is Cornwall really like? Is it just a playground for the rich tourist or a forgotten outpost in the Atlantic? Is it a land of pirates, myth and fantastic sun-kissed beaches, clotted cream teas and home of the (award winning) pasty or is it an exceptionally lonely and unforgiving place that's very wet in winter?

Having lived and worked in Cornwall for a number of years when I was fit and the rugged landscape was a major attraction I didn't need any other distractions – but now I find Cornwall still beautiful but very limited. Penzance, Truro and Falmouth are great, accessible places, and are worth anybody's time and I would urge all to visit them.

The Celts

The Cornish have made an industry out of 'The Celts'. Nobody has hazarded a guess as to how much it is worth but, like the pasty, there would be a significant hole in the county's economy if they weren't there.

So what is the truth? Did they exist or were they just a collection of unplaced people, a tribe, or were they indeed a proud race of warriors?

Academic writers report of a people from Eastern Europe around the Bronze Age, 13th century BC. Known as 'Urnfielders' they developed traits and characteristics later associated with the Celts. The Urnfielders seemed later to beget a tribe called the 'Cimmerians' who were more adventurous than the Urnfielders and in 700 BC they were swarming over the Hungarian plain to the Swiss lakes and into southern France and Belgium.

That is the closest to an origin, but the problem is that the Celtic 'race' is neither self-ascribed nor does it have any sense of national identity. Nobody who was a Celt ever talked about it.

The Romans put paid to most of the Celts. In this country, and at first hand, we can see how the Romans saw off a tribe known as the Durotiges who were happily settled in at Maiden Castle in Dorset. The Romans crushed them and then founded the town of Durnovaria (Dorchester). The thinking behind this was very good – near a river for water and more sheltered for housing. The Celts who did not pose a threat to the Romans either stayed at Maiden Castle or, seeing the civilised way the Romans conducted their life and the fact that housing was available, in a warmer place, and there was possible work to be had, they went the mile or so into Durnovaria. And that was about it for the Celts in Dorset. The Romans conquered Britain in 43 AD but did not stray too far into Cornwall, they traded with merchants but did not invade. The Romans also did not bother hugely with Wales or northern Scotland and it is these territories, these outposts that retain their links with the Celts.

The descriptions of what a Celt looked like tend to vary from LC Duncan-Jewell's 'short, squat, dark and swarthy' to the more Viking sounding 'light or red haired, tall and heroic'.

Whether they are a group/race/tribe started in Austrian salt mine villages, Greek, Turkey or somewhere in the Mediterranean no one really knows – it is up to the individual to speculate.

Saltash

The new **Celtic Cross** is going to be a 50ft high contemporary sculpture to greet people when crossing the Tamar. The project should have been completed by summer 2001 but either I was looking in the wrong direction or it hasn't actually been built. Saltash is often overlooked as people hurriedly surge across the Tamar and to be honest there isn't a lot here to make you stop. The whole area is dominated by Isambard Kingdom Brunel's wrought iron railway bridge – his last construction before his death – that was completed in 1859. The road bridge was opened in 1961. If you do stop, look out for a little cottage in **Culver Street**, which was Mary Newman's birthplace. She became the first wife of Sir Francis Drake and mayoress of Plymouth.

Population

15,576

Parking

Four disabled spaces. The town is on a slope, which is only to be expected as it is on the banks of the Tamar, and you will need help if you want to go exploring.

Park beside the main shopping street – it's closer than the car park – but there are no wheelchair accessible cafés.

Accommodation

● TRAVELODGE, Callington Road, Carkeel. Saltash Granada Service Area. 08700 850950. Two double

en-suite bedrooms for disabled. Next to Little Chef, which is accessible. www.travelodge.co.uk
- NOTTER MILL COUNTRY PARK, Notter Bridge, Saltash 01752 843694 One bungalow (of 23) equipped for wheelchair user. www.nottermill.co.uk
- CRYLLA VALLEY COTTAGES AND BUNGALOWS, Notter Bridge, Saltash 01752 851666.

Attractions

- ANTONY HOUSE (NT), Torpoint, Plymouth. 01752 812191. One of Cornwall's finest early 18th century houses. Views over Lynher river. Exclusive disabled parking spaces not far from reception. Café and shop accessible. The ground floor is accessible with a little help. The gardens have a preferred route but there are a few steps. Adapted disabled WC. www.nationaltrust.org.uk
- COTEHELE (NT), St Dominick, Saltash. 01579 351346. Help needed to get around the gardens and only the hall and kitchens are accessible – steeply sloping site but the café and shop are on the flat. Adapted disabled WC. www.nationaltrust.org.uk
- KERNOW MILL SHOPPING CENTRE, A38 roundabout heading towards Liskeard. Disabled parking spaces right beside the main entrance doors and it is level. Open seven days a week, a few shops selling clothes, sportswear, Edinburgh Woollen Mill (aren't they everywhere), shoes, gifts, a sort of Tourist Information Centre (TIC). There is a café – but it is up a flight of stairs and there is no lift. The toilets are on the lower level but it is not possible to get a wheelchair through the door.

There is a Little Chef close by, but that is not accessible because of three steps. Along the A38 dual carriageway there is a pleasant leafy layby that has toilets and disabled toilet and there is a van selling coffee. Kernow Mill is a good idea but let down by the inaccessible café and toilets.

- TAMAR CANOE EXPEDITION, Tinnel, Landulph, Saltash. 01579 351113. Canoe your way down the Tamar! Telephone first but wheelchair users have successfully used the canoes before.
- TAMAR CRUISES AND FERRY, Cremyll Ferry, Torpoint. 01752 822105. Ferry from Cornwall (Mount Edgcumbe) to Devon (Plymouth).

Comment
The town does little for wheelchair users.

East Looe

There are two Looes – one each side of the river. East Looe, the larger, is a bustling commercial resort linked to West Looe by a seven-arch Victorian bridge. In the last century huge amounts of granite and copper were shipped from the quay and today it still acts as a busy fishing port. Between Looe and Liskeard is the Duloe stone circle which comprises a small circle of massive white quartz stones which it is estimated, would not only have been very bright, but would have taken 40 people to lift.

Between Down Derry and Looe is a little beach called Seaton. The legend goes that Seaton was once a port larger than Plymouth but it was overwhelmed with sand because of a curse from a mermaid.

Population

5,180

Parking

The central/town centre car park has very few parking spaces and no disabled toilets. At the far end of the town (through the main shopping street) is an impressive looking toilet block with disabled toilet.

Accommodation

- TRELAWNE MANOR HOLIDAY PARK, Looe. 0870 242222. Haven holiday park with adapted caravans for wheelchair users. On site entertainment.
- GRANITE HENGE BUNGALOWS. 01503 272772. Eleven bungalows. Level access, swimming pool,

but no specific facilities for wheelchairs and some assistance needed. www.cornishcollection.co.uk/granitehenge.htm

- PENVITH BARN COTTAGES, St Martins by Looe. 01503 240772. Accessible but no facilities for disabled. www.cornwall-online.co.uk/penvith

Attractions

- OLD GUILDHALL MUSEUM, Higher Market Street. 01503 263709. Ground floor only accessible, and that is only by request!
- MONKEY SANCTUARY, Looe. 01503 262532. The ground slopes so take help, but there is an adapted disabled toilet.
- I-SPY GLASS BOTTOM BOAT, Banjo pier. 01503 263011. Limited access, help needed.

Eating and drinking

There are one or two cafés, which can be managed with some help.

Comment

Looe is a delightful looking town but it is just about inaccessible. The wheelchair user will need to be dropped off while a parking space is found, probably over the bridge at West Looe.

Liskeard

The economy in Liskeard boomed when copper was discovered around here in the 19th century. The town is located on top of a hill and used to be linked by canal to Looe. There is a pleasant and fairly level pedestrianised shopping street but the car parks are difficult. It's busy and popular with Plymouth commuters.

Population

8,190

Parking

The best, if an on street parking spot can't be found, is just off the centre on the higher side of town. Other car parks are on the western side and are long stay. Another is below Somerfield supermarket where there is no allocated disabled parking spaces but also no charge if displaying badge.

Accommodation

- RIVERVIEW VILLA. Fully accessible accommodation. Hoseasons Country Cottages. 01502 500500.
- DEER PARK FOREST CABINS, Herodsfoot. Forest Holidays. 0131 3146100. One, out of 46, adapted for wheelchair user.
- ROSECRADDOC LODGE, Liskeard. 01579 346768. Two adapted bungalows for wheelchairs. One has a bath, the other a shower.

Attractions

- DOBWALLS THEME AND ADVENTURE PARK. 0800 521812. Miniature railway, radio controlled boats, shooting gallery etc. Café, shops. Accessible, and free loan of wheelchair if required.
- QUAD AND KART CENTRE, Menheniot Station, Liskeard. 01579 347229. Accessible Quad bike racing and it has disabled WC.
- STERTS ARTS CENTRE, Upton Cross, Liskeard. 01579 362382. Open-air theatre, which has good disabled access to the main buildings. Art gallery, shop and café.
- LYNHER CHEESE FARM, Upton Cross, Liskeard. 01579362244. Working farm that is famous for Cornish Yarg cheese. Tour of milk parlour. Café, shop and picnic area. Help needed for access and there is no disabled WC.

Shopping (out of town)

- SAFEWAY superstore, towards St Austell/Bodmin. Disabled parking, café and toilets.
- TRAGO MILLS, many signposts on the Liskeard to Bodmin road point towards Trago Mills. Out of town shopping with great facilities for disabled. Level car park with many disabled spaces (always taken up by non-disabled!) and excellent disabled toilets. Shops, garden centre, café/restaurant, takeaway and cash machine. A very pleasant riverside setting.

Excellent purpose built shopping complex/village. *Highly recommended.*

Comment

A busy working town, which is not particularly attractive, built on a slope and with little to offer wheelchair users. Awkward.

Bodmin

The baton of county town status passed from Lostwithiel to Launceston to Bodmin and finally onto Truro were it now resides. In the 6th century Cornwall's patron saint, Petroc, arrived here from Padstow and founded his priory. The priory is no longer here but the 15th century church, the largest in Cornwall, probably occupies the same site.

Population

13,120

Parking

- PRIORY PARK is level and has toilets and disabled toilet together with allocated parking spaces.

Accommodation

- PENROSE BURDEN COTTAGES, St Breward. 01208 850277. Fully accessible converted farm buildings, but there are one or two modest slopes.

Attractions

- BODMIN AND WENFORD RAILWAY. Level fore-court parking, ramp to adapted railway coach. If possible please give 24hrs notice. 01208 73666.
- LANHYDROCK HOUSE AND GARDENS (NT). 01208 73320. This is one of the National Trust's prize attractions. A splendid Victorian country house with an estate of 900 acres. Close disabled parking which is useful as the main car park is quite a wheel/push. The majority of the ground floor is accessible via a ramp

and there is a small lift to the first floor. Some steps get in the way but generally with help it is accessible. Café and toilets. Outside there are smooth wheelchair paths alongside the Fowey River. A buggy is available if notice is given. www.nationaltrust.org.uk

- PENCARROW HOUSE AND GARDENS. 01208 841369. Most attractive Georgian house and listed gardens. Limited ground floor access with ramps etc. Close parking and disabled toilets. www.pencarrow.co.uk

Shopping

Part pedestrianised main shopping street, which is sloping.

Out-of-town shopping
Safeway superstore with allocated parking spaces, café and toilets. Asda superstore with parking, café and toilets.

Comment

It might have been Cornwall's capital once and it has the county's largest church but it has little to offer other than the supermarkets and steam railway.

Lostwithiel

Delightful riverside town with an interesting past. Once it was the sole port for Cornish tin and was only second to Southampton in terms of trade along the south coast and traded more tin than all the Cinque Ports (Sandwich, Dover, Hythe, Romney and Hastings) put together. Capital of Cornwall in the 13th century.

Population

2,569

Parking

The car park is in a lovely position beside the playing fields. It is free but has no allocated spaces or toilets. The other parking is set next to the River Fowey and level to the town's shops, which include a bakers and one or two restaurants that are level to access.

Accommodation

- BEST WESTERN RESTORMEL LODGE HOTEL, Lostwithiel. 01208 872223. One ground floor room equipped for wheelchair user.

Attractions

- RESTORMEL CASTLE (EH). This Norman castle is in good condition and was once home to Edward, the Black Prince. It's actually perched on a mound and although the views are good, access is very limited. www.english-heritage.org.uk

Comment

Another former capital of Cornwall. A charming, quiet and very attractive town, which is accessible.

Fowey

Fowey is an outstandingly beautiful place. Set at the mouth of the Fowey River with the town of Fowey on one side of the estuary and Polruan on the other. Fowey was a famous port in the middle ages and it still ranks as the 11th busiest port in the country with over one million tonnes of china clay exported each year. Fowey was Daphne Du Maurier's home town and she wrote her first novel, *The Loving Spirit*, here. Another writer and poet, the famous Cornishman, Sir Arthur Quiller-Couch is also from the town – he wrote *Dead Man's Rock* and *Hetty Wesley* plus many anthologies.

Population

2,130

Parking

- TOWER PARK car park near Readymoney Cove set at the top of the hill overlooking the town. Toilets and disabled toilets.

As expected with a gorgeous looking town such as Fowey, it is not the most accessible. Car parking within the town is either by trying to find an on road spot – these are few and far between – or, use the best car park at Station Road that is also used as a dinghy park. From here it is possible to wheel along to the shops a few hundred metres away and catch the wonderful views across the harbour. Although, because of the extra traffic in the summer months, visiting the town is difficult, it is definitely worth the effort!

Accommodation

- THE FOWEY HOTEL, The Esplanade, Fowey. 0800 243708. Accessible rooms, lift and parking. www.rich ardsonhotels.co.uk

Attractions

- HEADLAND GARDEN, Polruan-by-Fowey. 01726 870243. Limited access but there is an exclusive disa-bled-only car park.
- FOWEY RIVER STEAMERS, Town Quay. 01726 833278. Help available for access. *Recommended.* But telephone first to reserve seats.

Comment

Very pretty. It's not very wheelchair friendly, but it's still worth a visit.

Penzance

The Spanish burnt the town in 1565. At that time **Mouse-hole** was the main harbour on **Mount's Bay** but when it was rebuilt, Penzance became the dominant town. It is now a delightful and bustling market town with Cornwall's only promenade. Famous for being 'the end of the line' – from here you can only retrace your steps – Penzance is not a forgotten outpost but a charming and vibrant town. Just around the corner is Newlyn, which is the country's premier fishing port. Go there early in the morning to experience the fish sales and market. The Cornish have a fascination with capital towns and Penzance is known as 'the capital town of West Cornwall'.

Population

18,120

Parking

Flat, easy to find big car park with easy, level access to Wharfside Shopping Centre, which connects to the main shopping street. There is on-street parking, but the car park is available with three hours free if displaying badge and clock.

Accommodation

- THE GODOLPHIN ARMS, Marazion. 01736 710171. Two bedrooms have disabled access. www.godolphinarms.co.uk
- CHYMORVAH PRIVATE HOTEL, Marazion. 01736 710497. Accessible rooms.

Attractions

- TRINITY HOUSE NATIONAL LIGHTHOUSE CENTRE, Wharf Road. 01736 360077. The majority of exhibits are accessible, including the lighthouse quarters.
- TREREIFE, Penzance. 01736 362750. 18th century gardens. Limited wheelchair access. Tearoom.
- PENLEE HOUSE ART GALLERY AND MUSEUM, Morrab Road, Penzance. 01736 363625. Largest art collection in West Cornwall. Full wheelchair access.
- TREGWAINTON GARDEN (NT). 01736 363021. Exotic trees and shrubs in this sheltered subtropical garden. Strong help needed but it is accessible and wheelchairs are available. Tearoom and shop accessible. www.nationaltrust.org.uk
- MINACK THEATRE, Porthcurno, Penzance 01736 810694. Access is limited but it is worth a visit to this unique open-air theatre (full programme of plays every year) carved out of the rock. Ramped access from car park to entrance foyer, visitor centre, shop and café. Disabled toilet and ramp to disabled viewing balcony – incredible outlook! *Recommended.* www.minack.com
- LAND'S END, Sennen. 01736 871501. Dramatic landmark. Various attractions and facilities including the First and Last Inn, which dates back to 1620, the Land's End Pasty Parlour (I'm sure they are award-winning), and various restaurants and gift shops. There is also the Land's End Hotel. www.landsendlandmark.co.uk
- LAND'S END AERODROME, St Just, Penzance. 01736 7688771. Of course, the airfield is level but the planes can be difficult to enter. However, a trip around the headland is quite an experience especially if there is a puff of wind about. The stunning Minack Theatre

is even more impressive seen this way. If you've come this far, a flight is a must.

Look out for **Chapel Street** that connects the town centre to the harbour. A plaque at number 25 commemorates the home of Maria Branwell, the mother of Charlotte, Emily and Anne Bronte.

Shopping

There's a lift to the first floor of Wharfside Shopping Centre. Shops including Argos, a pet food shop, and several cafés and restaurants including a café and bar serving excellent espresso and cappuccino coffee on the balcony, and enjoying a wonderful outlook over Mounts Bay with views towards St Michael's Mount.

Along the main road are various local and national outlets including Wimpy, loads of art shops, and yet more 'award winning' pasty shops.

The town is a bit of a Mecca for all things Art, with galleries seemingly everywhere.

Head towards the west and the esplanade and beach are found. This is where the big hotels and amusements are located. The seafront is very impressive, with many long trips to be enjoyed, especially as there are purpose-built ramps for skaters and cyclists that wheelchair users can enjoy as well.

Out of town shops
- TESCO 24-hour superstore with allocated parking, café, disabled toilets and petrol station with fast card service.
- SAFEWAY superstore, allocated parking, café and disabled toilets.

Eating and drinking

- McDONALD'S drive-thru and restaurant. Nr Safeway on the A30. Disabled toilets.

Comment

A very pleasant surprise. Penzance is accessible and enjoyable and has the added attraction of so many unusual outlets.

St Ives

The town dates from the 5th century. The legend goes that St Ia floated into town on a leaf and established a settlement here. Very successful during the 18th century with a total of 19 mines in the area. Now the port and seaside resort is more famous for its artistic connections with links to Barbara Hepworth, Ben Nicholson, Bernard Leech and Henry Moore.

The importance of art is reflected in the opening of the Tate Gallery in 1993. The Tate is the place to be, and it is accessible although it looks impossible. Once inside there is a lift to take you to all the floors. If it can be managed, the roof café is the place for that cup of coffee.

Population

9,570

Parking

The best car park is by the beach at Porthmeor. Both car park and beach are small but very pleasant if a space can be found. In the summer, at the height of the season, St Ives is sometimes closed to cars.

Accommodation

- THE PORTHMINSTER HOTEL, The Terrace, St Ives. 01736 795221. Level car park. Adapted rooms, majority of hotel is accessible. Lift. Helpful staff. www.porthminster-hotel.co.uk

Attractions

- TATE GALLERY. 01736 796226. Steep ramp to access gallery, so help will be needed for this, but when inside a lift serves all floors including the roof top café, which has magnificent views. Shop. Adapted toilet. Wheelchairs available. *Highly recommended.* www.tate.org.uk
- ST IVES MUSEUM. 01736 796005. Harbourside location. Only about 50% is accessible.

Eating and drinking

- PORTHMEOR BEACH CAFÉ is opposite the Tate. The upstairs is accessible. There is limited parking along the road using blue/orange badge.

Comment

Interesting little place that's a bit overdone. However, it's worth a visit if only to sample the Tate's rooftop café.

Hayle

The 19th century was boom time for Hayle when it became a major industrial town supplying pumps and engines for the mining industry.

It's dull and flat but there are good wheels along the seafront to be enjoyed. There are three miles of sandy beaches and land speed sailing is carried out here.

Drive-thru McDonald's and restaurant within a group of facilities including Little Chef, petrol station, Brewsters large new family pub with Travel Inn accommodation.

Population

 7,650

Accommodation

- TRAVEL INN at Loggans Moor roundabout, Hayle. 01736 755025. Accessible bedrooms and en-suite bathrooms. Next to Loggans Moor Brewsters (Brewers Fayre). Parking spaces. www.travelinn.co.uk
- RIVIERE SANDS HOLIDAY PARK, Riviere Towans, Hayle. 01736 752132. Haven holiday park. Adapted caravan with shower. Entertainment facilities.

Attractions

- PARADISE PARK. Off A30 towards St Ives. 01736 757407. Rare bird collection. Shop, café and disabled toilets. Accessible.
- COUNTRY SKITTLES, Townshend, Hayle. 01736 850209. Off B3302 road to Helston. Ninepin bowling,

crazy golf, target rifle shooting and more! Some modest slopes but generally accessible. Bar and meals.

Comment

This is the first of a hat trick of dull north Cornwall towns, but it is accessible.

Camborne

Joined at the hip to Redruth. Another flat and dull town.

In the eighteenth century Camborne and Redruth were the richest mining area in the world. The Dulcoath mine was the most productive and deepest at 3,300 ft. Camborne's most famous son is engineer Richard Trevithick who was responsible for the high-pressure boiler and the Cornish beam engine.

Population

15,908

Parking

Parking on road or car parks. Rosewarne Car Park, which is just off the main shopping street. Small car park set to the west of this.

Accommodation

- TRAVEL INN at Carwin Rise, Hayle, next door to Loggans Moor Brewsters Fayre. 01736 755025. Two wheelchair accessible bedrooms with en-suite bathrooms, allocated disabled parking. www.travelinn.co.uk

Attractions

- ROWE BOWL, Trevithick Road, Camborne. 01209 711971. Tenpin bowling, amusements, pool, bar and family room. Level and accessible.
- CAMBORNE KARTING, Camborne. 01209 711993. Ramped access.

● CAMBORNE SCHOOL OF MINES, Pool. 01209 714866. Interesting collection of stones, rocks and minerals. The rooms are within the school and are well laid out for visitors. Level parking. www.ex.ac.uk

Shopping

 Argos and further shops are located in part-pedestrian-ised main shopping street. There is a Tesco superstore, with toilets, parking and fast card petrol station.

Comment

Like Redruth and Hayle, Camborne is accessible and if interested in finding out more about the mines of Cornwall, then pay a visit to Camborne School of Mines.

Redruth

Like so many west Cornish towns, Redruth never amounted to much prior to the mining boom of the 18th century.

Population

11,230

Parking

Large, level car park with disabled toilets and allocated spaces. Easy access to town centre.

Accommodation

- TRAVEL INN at Carwin Rise, Hayle. 01736 757029. Next to Loggans Moor Brewsters Fayre, accessible bedrooms with en-suite bathrooms and allocated disabled parking spaces.

Attractions

- TOLGUS TIN AND CORNISH GOLDSMITHS (road to Portreath). 01209 612142. Large level car park with concrete path to tin streaming and museum. Only small but very enjoyable. Pan for gold at Cornish Goldsmiths where there are disabled toilets. www.chycor.co.uk
- CORNISH MINES AND ENGINES, Pool. 01209 315027. Industrial Discovery Centre and Taylor's Engine House are accessible by lift.
- STITHIANS LAKE. 01209 860301. Water-skiing on this attractive lake is possible, also fishing and bird watching. Please telephone for details.

● ROSELAND HOUSE, Chacewater (east of Redruth). 01872 560451. Good access, tearoom, nursery, Victorian conservatory and unusual scented garden.

Shopping

 This is a miserable town but at least it is level and has a pleasant enough pedestrianised main shopping street.

Out of town shopping
McDonald's drive-thru, B&Q and Tesco at Tolgus Hill with allocated parking, café and disabled toilets. Petrol station with fast card. Safeway superstore. Disabled parking, café and toilets.

Comment
This is not a tourist destination, the area is steeped in Cornwall's rich mining past and some interesting attractions are fully accessible here. Tolgus Tin and Cornish Goldsmiths (with disabled toilets) are nearby and worth a visit.

St Agnes

A very pretty and accessible village. Although it is set on the more brutal north coast, the town has a softer look and feel to it.

Population

3,265

Parking

Set next to the beach, disabled toilets, parking spaces. Great position to sit, watch the waves and eat your award winning Cornish pasty.

Accommodation

- ROSE-IN-VALE COUNTRY HOUSE HOTEL, Mithian, St Agnes. 01872 552202. Three ground floor bedrooms, one with wide door to bathroom. www.rose-in-vale-hotel.co.uk

Attractions

- CORNISH GLIDING AND FLYING CLUB, Trevellas Airfield, St Georges Hill, Perranporth. 01872 572124. Please give some notice if flying is required.
- WORLD IN MINIATURE, Goonhavern, Perranporth. 01872 572828. Accessible. Gift shop, café, dodgems, and various attractions.

Shopping

- TREVANCE CRAFT WORKSHOP, which is accessible. There are some other shops, cafés and a hotel.

Truro

The main commercial centre of Cornwall. The capital and Cornwall's only city has an impressive three spire cathedral which is built on the site of the former St Mary's Church and was completed in 1910. It's set right in the heart of, and dominates, the centre. More than 800 years ago the town received its charter and ships still ply the Truro River which is formed from the confluence of rivers Kenwyn and Allen.

Population

16,870

Parking

The most obvious is the multi-storey car park that is located next to the cathedral. Lift and tarmac ramp gives access to main shopping street. Level, short stay car park close to the cathedral.

Accommodation

- TRAVEL INN, Cannon Downs. Three miles from Truro. 01872 863370. Next to Old Forge Brewsters. Allocated parking and accessible en-suite bedrooms. www.travelinn.co.uk
- ENGINE HOUSE (NT), Feock, Truro. 0870 458442. Adapted single storey property. www.nationaltrust.org.uk
- ELLWYN, Allet, Truro. 01872 277983. Country bungalow for 6/7 people. Suitable for disabled.

Comment

A very attractive small town, which is worth exploring.

Attractions

- TRURO BOWL, Moresk, Truro. 01872 222333. Accessible bowling centre with restaurant and bar.
- CALLESTOCK CIDER FARM. Penhallow. 01872 573356. Very pleasant working farm with excellent shop and café. Disabled toilets.

Shopping

A cobbled street leads to the main shopping street – it can be a bit of a pain to wheel along but it is worth the effort as there are some good shops here. The vast majority of the city centre shops are accessible. Truro flea market is also accessible, and next door to this is the TIC where you can obtain their disability pack detailing what is and what isn't accessible (not to be totally relied upon).

Out of town shopping
- TESCO, Garras Wharf. 24 hr. Disabled parking, café and toilets.

Eating and drinking

- CAFÉ UPSTAIRS DOWNSTAIRS serves good coffee and is just about accessible. It is down a little lane just off the main street.

Comment
Very friendly people, attractive city with good shops. Definitely the cultural centre of Cornwall.

Falmouth

Falmouth harbour and **Carrick Roads** form one of the finest, largest, deepest and most attractive harbours in the world. In the 16th century, Truro and Penryn were the main ports on the Fal estuary as they were more inland and easier to defend against marauding fleets of Spanish and French. **Falmouth Docks** now handles ships up to 90,000 tonnes. The town is also developing an international reputation as one of the best sailing and water sports centres in the world.

The town was granted Objective One status in 1999, the highest category of European structural funding for the 2000–2006 period. A new university is to be built in Cornwall with its campus in Falmouth.

Population

19,540

Parking

There is one car park at either end of the town. On the eastern (Truro) side is the smaller, moderately sloping car park, with two disabled spaces. It is very close to the main shopping street.

High Street is part pedestrianised and seems littered with cars parked using the orange/blue badge. The waterside car park has no disabled spaces but it does have the most tremendous views across Carrick Roads. It also has a steep slope to return to the High Street and help will be needed.

The other car park is to the western side of the High Street. It is a bit more relaxed, is flat and has disabled spaces and toilets with disabled toilet.

Accommodation

- ST ANTHONY HEAD (NT) (on the eastern side of Carrick Roads but only a short journey to Falmouth via King Harry Ferry). 0870 458442. Fully accessible ground floor cottage (one of four) with fantastic, uninterrupted views. www.nationaltrust.org.uk
- BROADMEAD HOTEL. 01326 315704. Centrally placed. Parking bay. Possible help needed.
- FALMOUTH BEACH RESORT HOTEL, Gyllingvase Beach. 01326 318084. A Best Western hotel. Lifts. Level entrance. Several rooms for disabled. Ground floor rooms give most space. Public rooms on ground floor. www.falmouthbeachhotel.co.uk

Attractions

- PENDENNIS CASTLE (EH). 01326 316594. Disabled parking. Access to grounds and keep. www.english-heritage.org.uk
- GLENDURGAN GARDENS (NT), Mawnan Smith. 01872 862090. Help needed if the gardens are to be explored but the café/tea house which serves excellent lunches and snacks is accessible. Disabled toilets and parking. www.nationaltrust.org.uk
- TREBAH, Mawnan Smith. 01326 250448. 25 acre sub tropical garden. Accessible. Café/tea house. Shop. www.trebah-garden.co.uk
- FALMOUTH FERRY, Prince of Wales Road. 01326 313201. Regular sailings to Frenchmans Creek, Helford etc. Assistance given.

- GYLLINGDUNE GARDENS AND PAVILION. 01326 311277. Phone for details of shows. Licensed bar and café. Disabled toilet.

Beaches
- GYLLINGVASE beach has a nice tarmac path around it, which leads to some formal gardens. There is a car park opposite the beach, or you can use the road for parking. Beach café and bar.
- SWANPOOL beach. Creek side tarmac path. Car park is level, beach café and toilets – but no disabled.
- MAENPORTH beach. Level parking. Bar/grill.

Shopping

The town is made up of multi branch shops which usually have good access and smaller private stores – they might not be particularly accessible but they are interesting.

Out of town shopping
- ASDA superstore. Allocated parking, toilets and café. Cash machine.

Eating and drinking

- If you can't get a coffee in town then a short journey to SHIPS AND LEGENDS will solve the problem. A recent and hugely impressive swimming pool and gym facility built on the side of a hill offers not only swimming but a pleasant café which is fully accessible and has disabled toilets together with allocated parking. Also there is a large grassed area for eating sandwiches and enjoying a picnic.

Comment

Very interesting town that combines being both a major tourist resort and a thriving marine business centre. There is more going on in Falmouth than other Cornish towns, which makes it a livelier place to stop.

Helston

Helston is famous for the **Helston Furry Dance** and for Bob Fitzsimmons, Britain's first world heavyweight boxing champion who won his crown in the 19th century. In the 13th century, the stannary town of Helston was a port exporting copper and tin before it was cut off from the sea at **Loe Bar** – no mention of spiteful mermaids so it must have been a natural occurrence.

Population

9,450

Parking

- TRENGROUSE WAY is the main car park and it is on a steep slope so strong help will be needed. Lower Trengrouse has two disabled spaces but the main shopping street – Meneage Street – is only accessed via a steep pathway.
- WENDON STREET car park is level and is set off one of the main through roads.

There are various on street parking spots around the town.

Accommodation

- PENZANCE ROAD LODGE, Ashton. 01736 763217. Single storey motel. Allocated parking. Bedrooms suitable for disabled.
- ELM, Cadgwith, Ruan Minor, Helston (NT). 0870 4584422. Accessible, single storey, two bedroom

cottage. No shower cubicle or disabled toilet but there are some great views! www.nationaltrust.org.uk

Attractions

- FLAMBARDS THEME PARK. 01326 564093. Very successful family attraction. Set on a slope so help needed. Good close allocated parking, someone needed to hold on as you make your descent to the park. Disabled toilets, restaurants and cafés – all accessible. It's big, bright and brash. www.flambards.co.uk
- THE NATIONAL SEAL SANCTUARY, Gweek. 01326 221874. Allocated parking very close to entrance. Steeply sloping site but also very enjoyable. A fully accessible Land Rover pulled trailer takes visitors to the pools. Sea lions and seals. Shop and café. Disabled toilets. www.sealsanctuary.co.uk
- GOONHILLY EARTH STATION, The Lizard. 0800 679593. Extensively fitted shop with all things 'space'. Interactive games, large accessible café, disabled toilets and allocated parking but the tour bus is not currently accessible. www.goonhilly.bt.com

Shopping

- SOMERFIELD supermarket is located by the Trengrouse car park and has disabled parking spaces.
- TESCO 24hr superstore (off the main road to the Lizard) has disabled parking spaces, café and disabled toilets. Petrol station with fast card.

Comment

No café within the town centre and both Meneage and Coinagehall Street are steep so help will be needed.

St Austell

Big touring centre and busy, thriving town. Famed for its china clay quarries and 'moonscape' vista. Now just as famous for **The Eden Project**, the vast greenhouses occupying what used to be one of the china clay quarries. In the mid-nineteenth century over 7,000 people were employed in china clay extraction and processing. It is still one of Cornwall's big employers and exporter world wide.

Population

21,360

Parking

The town centre is pedestrianised but unfortunately it is difficult to get to. The car park, or nearest car park, is on some steep sloping ground and it makes access to the main shops very awkward. Help definitely required.

Accommodation

- SEAPOINT HOUSE HOTEL, Mevagissey 01726 842684. Accessible room with direct access from car park.
- CARLYON BAY HOTEL. 01726 812304. Luxury hotel but with limited facilities for wheelchair users. www.carlyonbay.co.uk

Attractions

- THE EDEN PROJECT, St Austell. Major tourist attraction, which cost about £85 million. Two gigantic greenhouses (one more soon to be added) and two very large cafés. There is a bit more to it than that and be prepared to spend several hours there. Although it seems to have been built on the side of a disused volcano the attraction is very accessible. There are excellent staff there to offer any assistance needed. The Eden Project is accepting awards left, right and centre and even mentioned as one of the wonders of the world. It has, on its own, regenerated the tourist economy in this part of Cornwall. Without the support and forward thinking from the local council – who put up some venture capital when it was at a critical stage – the project would not have happened. Go and see what all the fuss is about. There are great facilities for wheelchair users but take someone with you who can push so that everything can be seen.

- LOST GARDENS OF HELIGAN, St Austell. 01726 844157. Tim Smit is the man behind both Lost Gardens of Heligan and The Eden Project and he does have a brilliant knack for titles. Excellent restored gardens. Although not all the garden is accessible it is definitely worth visiting. Allocated parking, great café/restaurant, and disabled toilets.
- AUTOMOBILIA, The Old Mill, St Stephen, St Austell. 01726 823092. Early 20th century cars. It is 80% accessible, with a model shop, gifts and café.
- CORNISH MARKET WORLD, Stadium Retail Park, St Austell 01726 815553. Only operates at the weekend. Large indoor market full of traders selling everything you'd expect at a market. Large level car park with disabled spaces. Easy access and everything is accessible throughout the market. Stalls include many catering establishments – bakers, butchers, delicatessen and outside are two or three large takeaway vans. Disabled toilets. Cash machine. Outdoor children's play area. It is a very accessible venue and fine if you like markets.

- OZZELL BOWL, Priory Car Park, Priory Road, St Austell. 01726 77766. Tenpin bowling for the whole family. Good accessibility, easy parking, restaurant and disabled toilets. www.ozzellbowl.co.uk
- COLISEUM BEACH COMPLEX. This comprises a nightclub, restaurant, grill and bar. Set right on the beach with large, level car park. This used to be Carly-on Bay beach but it has now become Coliseum beach, it was tacky before and still is.

Shopping (out of town)

- TESCO 24hr with disabled parking, café and toilets. Petrol station with fast card.
- ASDA with disabled parking, café and toilets. Cash machine.
- McDONALD'S drive-thru and restaurant with disabled toilets.
- LITTLE CHEF WITH BURGER KING – café, restaurant, takeaway and disabled toilets.

Comment

It's a shame there are no car parking facilities close enough to the shops and town centre.

Charlestown

Developed as a working port in the 18th century for the china clay industry and now favoured as a film location. Good wheelchair access and disabled toilets. Café, exhibits and the largest shipwreck artefact collection in Britain.

Population

21,360 (including St Austell)

Parking

Two allocated parking spaces.

Attraction

- SHIPWRECK AND HERITAGE CENTRE, Quay Road, Charlestown, St Austell. 01726 69897. www.shipwreckcharlestown.com

Eating and drinking

- BOSUNS BISTRO. Café/restaurant. Wheelchair access and toilet.

Comment

Charlestown is well known as a TV and film set and has the popular Heritage Centre. Also there is an outdoor pursuit site that is wheelchair accessible.

Launceston

Yet another former capital town (until 1835 when the honour went to Bodmin). Located on the far eastern boundaries of Cornwall, this is a pleasant enough place and there isn't the panic of trying to find some change as you cross the Tamar at Plymouth. The town is dominated by the remains of a Norman castle stuck on the highest point at Dunheved. The castle was the seat of The Earl of Cornwall but only the outer bailey is accessible for wheelchair users.

Population

7,030

Parking

The best car park is the one at the heart of the town, surrounded by shops. The trouble is, everyone wants to park there, but the alternatives are some way away from the centre and you would come across some steep hills, so it is best to keep circling around like a vulture waiting for a space.

Whilst you are there enjoy the limited, but reasonably accessible, shopping facilities. The town was built up around the Norman castle and of course castles are usually built on top of a hill.

Accommodation

- TRAVELODGE, Okehampton. 0800 850 950. This is the most accessible place to stay.

Attractions

- TRETHORNE LEISURE FARM, Kennards House, Launceston. 01566 86324. Three miles west, off A30. Family attraction with loads to do. It is mostly accessible but the roller blading isn't! Café, undercover picnic area, disabled toilets.
- LAUNCESTON STEAM RAILWAY. Off A30 (signposted). Ingenious method to accommodate wheelchairs onto train, you must try it. Café.

Shopping (out of town)

- TESCO with disabled parking, café and toilets. Petrol station with fast card.

Comment

The hill restricts but there are some interesting shops in the centre.

Bude

Just about clinging onto Cornwall, this north Cornish town has all the attributes and feel of Devon. Bude is a popular family resort, famed for its surfing and beaches. In Victorian times it was the subject of major canal construction to link the upper Tamar with the Bristol Channel, thus making Cornwall an island. The railways arrived and the venture was dropped.

Population

7,420

Parking

On the eastern side of Bude town centre are the SUMMERLEAZE and CROOKLETS car parks. Both are large and level and both have toilets and disabled toilets. The Crooklets car park enjoys a fantastic position with views over the sea. To the west lies LOWER WHARF car park, which is level and has a tarmac surface. Within the car park is the TIC, which is fully accessible with ramps and automatic doors. Next to the TIC is a toilet block with disabled toilet and allocated disabled parking.

Local council offices are also here together with the Fire Station, school and the Bude–Stratton museum.

Accommodation

● HARTLAND HOTEL, Bude. 01288 355661. Heated swimming pool, lift and all bedrooms en-suite. No

specific disabled facilities but the doors are wide enough to accommodate a wheelchair.
- SHARLANDS FARM, Marhamchurch. 01288 362322. Single storey, two bedroom barn conversion.

Attractions

- THE BUDE–STRATTON MUSEUM, The Castle. 01288 353576. Limited seasonal opening times. Accessible but some help may be required.
- UPPER TAMAR LAKE. 01288 321262. Watersports centre. Café and shop. Accessible but some help will be required.

There are some excellent, level walks alongside the river and beach (bracing). There are further walks along the network of canals (level).

Eating and drinking

Beach café (seasonal), licensed restaurant at Lower Wharf car park with indoor and outdoor seating (no disabled toilets), town centre café and Coffee Pot café to the east of the centre (no disabled toilets). Safeway supermarket café with disabled parking and disabled toilets.

Shopping

Town centre shopping is mostly seasonal fare. One or two have reasonable access with limited on-street parking outside.

Out of town shopping

- SAFEWAY supermarket with disabled parking, café and toilets. Petrol station.

Comment

More like a north Devon resort than north Cornwall but as the border is only four miles away that is understandable. It offers a great deal for wheelchair users and is a delightful and charming place.

Newquay

Brash and tacky it might be (Cornwall's Ibiza so the brochures say!) but it is Cornwall's biggest seaside resort. Seven miles of sand and 11 beaches. Until 1998 the World Surfing Championships were held here every summer. Now they are held in France.

Near The Atlantic Hotel stands the little **Huer's House**, a watchtower, from where the huer kept a watch out for approaching pilchard shoals. Apparently, in 1868 at St Ives, there was a record catch of 16.5 million fish. The most famous beach of the several here is **Fistral Beach**, which is a Mecca for surfers. You can park on the sand and there are toilets with disabled facilities. If you want a quieter place to dabble your toes try **Towan** or **Tolcarne** beach.

Population

18,780

Parking

Parking is best at THE MANOR car park, which has disabled spaces and is close to the centre. For a slightly more sophisticated side head for the Pitch and Putt course which has a car park and a small café serving tea/coffee. This has a pleasant park-like setting. Follow signs for the zoo if you want to visit this.

Accommodation

• HEADLAND HOTEL. 01637 872211. Imposing 100 bedroom hotel at Fistral Beach. Disabled toilet, ramps for access and lift to all floors but no full facilities in bedrooms. www.headlandhotel.co.uk

- TREGARN HOTEL, Pentire. 01637 874292. Lift, car park and ground floor room but no specific facilities.

Attractions

- NEWQUAY ZOO, Trenance Leisure Park. 01637 873342. Cornwall's only zoo has lions, pumas and other exotic animals. It is accessible and has two sets of disabled toilets at either end of the zoo, not far from the Pitch and Putt course. Café and shop. www.newquayzoo.co.uk
- NEWQUAY SEA LIFE CENTRE, Towan Promenade. 01637 872822. Over 30 displays. Café, gift shop. Disabled toilets and lift.
- DAIRYLAND FARM WORLD, Summercourt. 01872 510349. Heritage centre, pony rides, loads of animals, gift shop, disabled toilets, wide doors and ramps.
- TRERICE, near Newquay (NT). 01637 875404. Elizabethan manor and gardens. Parking close to house – ring first. Tea room and shop accessible. Ground and first floor (via grass slope) accessible in house. Limited access to gardens. www.nationaltrust.org.uk
- CARNEWAS AND BEDRUTHAN STEPS (NT), a few miles further east of Newquay. Car park. The views from here are outstanding. The ground is relatively level although the actual path is a bit bumpy. The north Cornish coast does have some incredible coastal views and some of them are here. Café with indoor or outdoor seating.

The National Trust do their best for wheelchair users, the many sided fixed outdoor tables and seating having one section cut away with a plaque fitted saying 'Wheelchair'! They treat you like their best friend and the coffee and cakes are excellent. *Highly recommended.* www.nationaltrust.org.uk

Beaches
From the town centre, travel east to find some delightful small beaches. Most have their own car parks.

- PORTH BEACH has a level car park with a small parade of shops and an accessible pub.
- WATERGATE BAY. Sand and tarmac car park, which is level and has toilets with disabled toilet. Moderate slope to the beach.
- MAWGAN PORTH. Car park, level to beach. Café and shop that have been made as accessible as possible for wheelchairs including a disabled parking place for five minutes – the shop's not very big. Main car park has toilets and disabled toilet.

Shopping

 The town centre offers the usual seaside resort goodies with amusements, takeaways, Burger King and gift shops. You don't really come to Newquay for shopping. There is a SOMERFIELD supermarket, which has its own car park.

Comment
Tacky, tatty and very difficult to find anywhere suitable for a wheelchair user but there are accessible parts.

Padstow

Exceptionally pretty estuary town and harbour named after the Cornish saint, Petroc, who established a monastery and the town (Petrockstow) here in the 6th century. Famous now as the home of TV chef Rick Stein who has various restaurants in the town – his popularity has led some locals to rename the town 'Padstein'.

The mermaid's tale is a legend that tells the story of how Padstow used to be a great port with water deep enough for the largest vessel, and was under the care of a merry maid, but one day when she was frolicking in the water she was shot and she was rightly upset and vowed that henceforth the harbour should be desolate. The moral of this sad tale? Never shoot a frolicking mermaid.

Population

2,550

Parking

On the main road into Padstow is the main car park, but this is at the top of the hill and we don't want that. It does, however, have toilets and a disabled toilet.

Another car park at a more realistic level is by the harbour.

It is easy to get around the town as most of it is beside the harbour. Pubs, cafés, takeaways etc. are mostly accessible – Rick Stein owns most of them, so complain to him if you have problems.

Accommodation

- METROPOLE HOTEL. 0870 4008122. Built for the railway (which isn't there anymore). Two bedrooms suitable for wheelchair user. Dining room has lovely views overlooking estuary.

Attractions

- PRIDEAUX PLACE, Padstow. 01841 532411. Elizabethan Manor. Access only to ground floor and tearooms.
- THE CAMEL TRAIL, which is accessible for wheelchairs, travels between Padstow and Wadebridge. As it is a former railway line it is level and runs for about four miles. Fantastic scenery, either start here by the main lower level car park or at Wadebridge.
- THE PADSTOW HOBBY HORSE is a Celtic tradition performed here every 1 May. A wheel to the end of the pier/harbour wall. If you time it right, a ferry trip to Rock on the other side of the estuary is well worth it. The blokes running the boat are very good and will help wherever possible but you will have to negotiate some steps (make sure your return journey will land you back by the steps, if you leave it too late the alternative landing spot is impossible with a wheelchair).

Shopping (out of town)

- TESCO located on the outskirts heading towards Wadebridge, disabled parking, café, toilets and cash machine.

Comment

An extremely pretty town and well worth exploring if a parking space can be found.

Wadebridge

The town used to be called simply Wade when there was a ford to cross the Camel. In the 1460s a bridge was constructed and, because the sand was swallowing up all stone foundations put down, it is said packs of wool were used instead. Some major town centre redevelopment has turned Wadebridge into one of the most accessible towns visited; it's always been a lovely place but now it can be enjoyed even more. It lies beside the river and now has some excellent wheels alongside it.

Population

5,930

Parking

Tarmac surface, level, central and giving direct access to the pedestrianised main shopping street (slight slope).

Toilets

● EGLOSHAYLE ROAD (to Bodmin) with disabled toilets.

Accommodation

● ST MINVER HOLIDAY PARK, St Minver. 01208 862305. Haven holiday park. Caravans for five people adapted for disabled guests.

Attractions

● SHIRES ADVENTURE PARK, Trelow Farm, Wadebridge. 01841 540276. Accessible shire-horse attraction with many other animals. Craft and gift shop. Restaurant.

- MELLINGEY MILL WILLOW CRAFT CENTRE, St Issey, Wadebridge. 01841 540604. The majority of this attraction is accessible. Craft shop, willow basket showroom.
- DELABOLE WIND FARM, Delabole, North Cornwall. 01840 213377. This wind farm – Cornwall's first – was established in 1991. Level car park but no facilities. It's quite an eerie place. When the wind is up it is even more impressive, if not slightly surreal, as the arms move quietly and efficiently chopping through the atmosphere. Cornwall has a number of wind farms and other sites can be seen on hilltops looking like they're gathering, ready to take over the world – Don Quixote did warn us!

Shopping

- PIONEER supermarket with two allocated parking spaces.
- LIDL supermarket with disabled parking spaces.

Quite a network of businesses has developed around the Camel Trail. Shops include a cycle hire shop that does have bikes for those with limited mobility/strength (tel: 01208 813050). The Oasis café, also by the Camel Trail start/finish, has outdoor seating.

Out of town shopping
- TESCO on the road to Padstow. Disabled parking, toilets and café. Two ATM cash machines outside.

Eating and drinking

- FISH AND CHIPS close to the 'Bridge on Wool', either eat in or out.

Comment

Wadebridge is only a small town and yet it offers excellent facilities for a wheelchair user. The town centre is level, well laid out and has the advantage of a pedestrianised main shopping street. A park-like grassed area beside the river provides enjoyable wheels/walks. The Camel Trail is worth trying either by hopping onto a bike or using your wheelchair. *Recommended.*

Index of Attractions within their Counties

Devon